1000 Best Poker Strategies and Secrets

Susie Isaacs

SOURCEBOOKS, INC.®
NAPERVILLE, ILLINOIS

FEB - 1 2007

Copyright © 2006 by Susie Isaacs
Cover and internal design © 2006 by Sourcebooks, Inc.
Sourcebooks and the colophon are registered trademarks of
Sourcebooks, Inc.

This publication is designed to provide accurate and author-
itative information in regard to the subject matter covered. It
is sold with the understanding that the publisher is not
engaged in rendering legal, accounting, or other professional
service. If legal advice or other expert assistance is required,
the services of a competent professional person should be
sought.—*From a Declaration of Principles Jointly Adopted by
a Committee of the American Bar Association and a Committee of Publishers and Associations*

Published by Sourcebooks, Inc.
P.O. Box 4410, Naperville, Illinois 60567-4410
(630) 961-3900
Fax: (630) 961-2168
www.sourcebooks.com

Library of Congress Cataloging-in-Publication Data

Isaacs, Susie.
  1000 best poker strategies and secrets / Susie Isaacs.
      p. cm.
  Includes bibliographical references.
  ISBN-13: 978-1-4022-0668-9
  ISBN-10: 1-4022-0668-2
  1. Poker. I. Title: One thousand poker strategies and secrets.
II. Title.
  GV1251.I83 2006
  795.412—dc22
                        2005033345

Printed and bound in Canada.
WC 10 9 8 7 6 5 4 3 2 1

Contents

Acknowledgments vii

Introduction xi

Poker Basics 1

Glossary 7

1: Limit Texas Hold'em 23

2: No-Limit Texas Hold'em .83

3: Seven-Card Stud 143

4: Razz 175

5: Seven-Card Stud High-
   Low Split Eight-or-Better 189

6: Omaha 211

7: Omaha High-Low Split Eight-or-Better 225

8: Five-Card Draw Jacks-or-Better,
   Jacks-Back, and Lowball Draw 245

9: Tells 263

10: Home Games 275

11: Internet Poker 287

12: Brick-and-Mortar Card Casinos
    and Poker Rooms 311

13: Poker Table Protocol 329

14: My Friends Give Big Tips 345

Bibliography 377

About the Author 379

Dedication

This book is dedicated to my mom, "Mimi." She never played a hand of poker in her life, but she was my biggest fan.

Acknowledgments

Since I began this project, my list of appreciation for certain individuals has grown almost daily. It isn't easy to write a book, even if writing and the subject matter you are writing about is your passion, especially if the information is sometimes technical. It is so important to get the details correct if your hope is to direct others in their passion or in their pursuit to learn and excel in a multifaceted subject. One misdirection—one "do" when you shouldn't, or one "don't" when you should—could end in ultimate confusion. I believe with the help, suggestions, corrections, and directions of a bunch of good folks, this work resulted in a great book.

If I have forgotten anyone, I'll run down the Las Vegas Strip naked (in my next life!).

Thank you Jessica Faust, my literary agent from Book Ends, Inc., for finding me. You led me out of the darkness of "What do I do now?" to the light of a publisher, Sourcebooks, Inc.

Thank you Sourcebooks, Inc. for gambling on me. Although lots of people, especially poker people, know me, I was a virtual unknown in the world of publishing.

Maryann Guberman, my poker editor, thank you for making me look totally literate. I know that time is a precious commodity and I appreciate your making enough of it to help me out with this project.

Ewurama Ewusi-Mensah, thank you for your time and efforts in polishing this manuscript. If you weren't a poker player before, you are now!

Michelle Schoob, thank you for checking and rechecking my poker terminology. I don't know if every writer needs multiple editors, but I sure did!

Thank you Herminia Mahealani Suzanna Sniffen (that's why we call her "Hermie"), my business partner, for carrying the load and being so patient while I buried myself in this project.

Thank you Darlene Wood, my friend and my research assistant. If it weren't for you, this would have taken me twice as long.

Thank you Linda Johnson for believing in me and pointing me in the right direction.

Thank you Jan Fisher for explaining the theory on the calculations of odds, outs, and percentages in terms a regular person can grasp.

Thank you June Field for your wisdom and for opening the first poker publishing opportunity for me through the pages of *Card Player* magazine and *Poker Digest*.

Thank you: Dan Harrington, author of *Harrington on Hold'em*; John Vorhaus, author of *Killer Poker Online*; George Elias, author of *Awesome Profits*; Bill Burton, author of *Get the Edge at Low-Limit Texas Hold'em* and *1000 Best Casino Gambling Secrets*; Matthew Hilger, author of *Internet Texas Hold'em*;

and Shane Smith, author of *Omaha Hi-Lo Poker (Eight or Better) How to Win at the Lower Limits,* for your tips that made this book stronger.

Thank you Dana Smith for your unselfish cooperation and knowledge when I hit a weak link.

Thank you Rick Gianti, even though you're not working in poker any longer, you'll always have poker in your blood and your heart.

Thank you a "stack of black," my poker champion friends, for enhancing this work with your poker wisdom: Doyle Brunson, Todd Brunson, Vince Burgio, Mike Caro, Johnny Chan, T. J. Cloutier, Barbara Enright, Barry Greenstein, Maureen Feduniak, Phil Gordon, Russ Hamilton, Tom McEvoy, Howard Lederer, Daniel Negreanu, Scotty Nguyen, Greg Raymer, Mike Sexton, Dr. Max Stern, and Robert Williamson—you're all the "nuts"!

Introduction

In the days of the Old West, fistfights or even gunfights often settled disputes. A century later, folklore has it that characters accused of unsavory poker conduct could be found buried in the desert. Through it all, home poker games have prevailed. Those who participated were not part of the criminal element. They were regular folks who enjoyed a great mind-exercising game of cards. The poker renaissance that began just a few years ago has evolved into the greatest phenomenon in recent memory. Poker tournaments, popular among an elite group of competitors since the seventies, now draw thousands of newcomers from all walks of life. The World Series of Poker, the granddaddy of all poker competitions and the biggest and most prestigious poker tournament for over thirty years, grew slowly but steadily every year. It was the single richest competition the game ever saw. Today, multimillion-dollar poker competitions are commonplace and are being played all over the world. You might say that the game of poker and its reputation have gone from the outhouse to the penthouse in only a few hundred years. What happened? A series of auspicious events took place that culminated with poker competition rising to become a "top of the ratings chart" new spectator sport. First, a group of poker-loving poker players had a vision in the jungle. Honest! While Mike Sexton, Linda Johnson, and Steve Lipscomb vacationed in Costa Rica in 2000, they discussed their common interest and love of the game. Steve shared his vision for a concept called the World Poker Tour. All Steve needed was funding. Mike was associated with Party Poker (one of the first and today one of the largest online poker sites), which was a nice fit, and this Internet giant ultimately became a charter member. Linda owned *Card Player* magazine and Card Player Cruises. The trio, Sexton, Lipscomb, and Johnson, went to see Lyle Berman (poker player extraordinaire and owner of Lakes Entertainment) when they returned to Las Vegas. Berman listened to their fantasy and said that they would need six or eight charter members—casinos or online poker sites willing to participate. Before he committed to his part in the big plan, Berman gave them a deadline of six months to find six sponsors willing to bet on the come, so to speak. They got their participating charter members in six weeks and the deal was on!

The World Poker Tour was a success from the first season it aired in 2002 on the Travel Channel. The brainstorm that turned poker into a true spectator sport was the tiny "lipstick" cameras built into the poker table. Poker has been televised for years, but it was about as exciting as watching a dog sleep. Suddenly, the ability to know what cards the players were holding and to watch how they interacted with each other, bet, and bluffed, opened a totally new frontier. Poker was downright exciting, and its popularity exploded!

Three dedicated poker players really thought the World Poker Tour would be a homerun, and it turned out to be a grand slam! The poker world is forever changed because of these three visionaries in the jungle.

The next giant step in the unbelievable growth of poker popularity came about on May 24, 2003, when a young man from Nashville, Tennessee, named Chris Moneymaker (his real name!) won the coveted World Series of Poker title and an unbelievable $2.5 million. Prior to his first visit to Las Vegas and his first "live" poker tournament, he was not a wealthy man. He was an accountant and a family man, the guy next door, and a breadwinner.

Through the years anyone in a financial position to shell out $10,000 could have the privilege of matching wits with the best poker players in the world. Moneymaker, just a regular guy, won his seat in an online poker competition that cost him a mere $40. The popularity and acceptance of a game that once was frowned upon by a large segment of the population experienced a complete metamorphosis. Moneymaker was a huge piece in this phenomenal poker puzzle. Overnight he became to poker what Tiger Woods is to golf and Bill Gates is to computers.

The following year, 2004, another everyman and online qualifier, Greg Raymer, won the title and $5 million! This really put the icing on the poker cake. It proved that Moneymaker's feat wasn't a fluke; it could and did happen again. Long shots do come in. It is now a matter of record that anyone with some poker skill, luck at the right times, an ability to bluff but avoid being bluffed, and a lot of patience and heart can become a millionaire—or at least a thousandaire—through poker.

Though it has reached a new pinnacle over the last few years, poker is and always has been a sport of skill that also happens to be fun, and a great social activity for the masses. Learning how to play poker properly is easy with the advent of Internet poker to practice in private and televised poker competitions to watch and enjoy. Online poker sites and public casinos and cardrooms offer every individual the opportunity to learn to play poker correctly. However, in order to excel in your private poker games or compete in the big time, you'll need certain tools. *1000 Best Poker Strategies and Secrets* will pave the way to acquiring the skills and knowledge that will help you win.

Over the years there have been a wide variety of poker games to incorporate into your poker repertoire from silly wild card and poker drinking games (so you don't care if you win or lose) to the real poker games that can be mastered. In this book, we're going to concentrate on the most popular games played in brick-and-mortar poker emporiums (casinos and cardrooms) and online poker sites as well as some that are not easy to find in a casino, cardroom, or online but are great games to play at home. If you are a beginner who wants to learn how to stop losing (at the very least) and learn how to win, an intermediate player who wants to improve his game and win more, or an advanced player who wants to reinforce and define his game, this book is for you. It also may introduce you to some real poker games that you are not familiar with but will enjoy playing. There is a lot more to poker than the no-limit games you watch on TV.

We will cover the following games:

- Limit Texas hold'em: a flop game in which each player receives two hole (private) cards to go with five community cards. Each player makes the best five-card hand out of the seven cards.
- No-limit Texas hold'em: the basics are the same as limit hold'em except you can bet any amount at any time. It's the same as limit Texas hold'em, only different! Sounds simple, but it isn't!
- Omaha: another flop game where each player receives four hole cards to work with.
- Omaha high-low split: begins like Omaha but with a twist that lets you play for the highest hand, the lowest hand, or both. (To win both ways is to "scoop" the pot.)
- Seven-card stud: a favorite and a staple for most who know poker. In seven-card stud players receive two downcards, four upcards, and one more down. (There are no community cards in stud games. Each player receives his own seven cards to make the best five-card hand.)
- Razz: like seven-card stud, except you play for the best low hand rather than the best high.

- Seven-card stud high-low split: similar to seven-card stud, but with the same two-way twist as Omaha high-low. Stud high-low is sort of a combination of seven-card stud and razz, a real thinking (wo)man's game.
- I also will give you the ins and outs of a few California cardroom games that were once very popular: five-card draw with a joker, jacks-back, and lowball.

With the exception of draw poker, jacks-back, and lowball, each chapter on each of the aforementioned games will be divided into subsections: tips for the beginner, tips for the intermediate, and tips for the advanced player.

For those of you who want to go a little deeper and get more information on the psychological aspects of poker, the chapter on tells will take you to the next step in becoming a winning player. Poker is as much about playing the people as it is about playing your cards.

We will discuss home games. If you already host a home game, you may pick up some fresh ideas for fun and profit within the pages of this chapter. We'll also discuss playing poker on the Internet for fun, practice, and profit and how to make a smooth transition from your home to real brick-and-mortar poker emporiums.

The majority of you who decided to purchase this book will have a basic understanding of the language of poker. You know at least the most common terms, the flop (the first three community cards), the turn (the fourth card), and the river (the fifth). There is so much more poker jargon that you will have a much easier time gaining a full understanding of the upcoming tips if you familiarize yourself up front with the glossary. If you come across a word in the tips that causes you to scratch your head and say, "Huh?" just check out the glossary for a full understanding. I'm not only going to teach you how to become a better poker player, you're going to get a bonus; you'll also be learning another language!

Keep one thing in mind as you develop your own winning style; the best poker players in the world will have losing days and the worst poker players in the world will experience winning days. There is no other sport in the world where this can happen so dramatically. But keep in mind that the cream will rise to the top.

If you have the desire, the patience, the drive, the heart, and the determination, maybe—just maybe—someday you'll find yourself at the final table of a major poker tournament, rubbing elbows with the poker stars! Please tell them I sent you.

Last, but certainly not least, I'll have a chapter of tips, comments, and opinions from some of the superstars in the wonderful world of poker who I have had the privilege of meeting through the years.

Poker Basics

The Goal

In poker, your goal is to make the right decisions—whether to call, fold, check, raise, or reraise—so that at the end of each hand you are either the holder of the winning hand or the last (wo)man standing—*or* if you lose the hand, you lose as little as possible. Correct decisions (sometimes coupled with some luck) will determine the overall winner. By overall winner, I mean that although you may lose some sessions or some tournaments, when you continually make the correct decisions, at the end of the year, the cream—you!—will rise to the top.

Table Layout

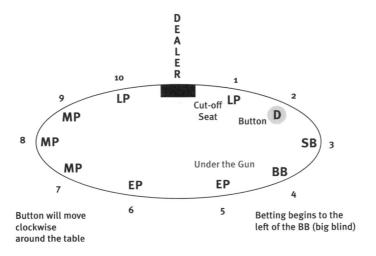

D: Dealer button
SB: Small blind
BB: Big blind
EP: Early position
MP: Middle position
LP: Late position

Hand Rankings

Remember, the winning hand is made up of the best five cards (see below for rankings). You may use one or two of your hole cards in conjunction with three or four of the community cards in hold'em; in Omaha you must use two of your hole cards.

| Low Cards | Be gone |
| Highest Card | Be lucky |

One Pair	Be careful
Two Pair	Be ready to bet your ballpoint pen
Three of a Kind	Be ready to bet your toaster
Straight	Be ready to bet your stereo
Flush	Be ready to bet your Schwinn
Full House	Be ready to bet your Geo
Four of a Kind	Be ready to bet your Mercedes
Straight Flush	Be ready to bet your yacht
Royal Flush	Bet the ranch and the cattle

In some poker games such as razz and Omaha high-low, players attempt to make low hands. See "A Note about Low Hands" in chapter 4, "Razz," for an explanation of how low hands are ranked.

Nine Fundamentals Every Poker Player Should Understand

Becoming a winning poker player takes a wealth of knowledge and hundreds of hours of practice. There is no shortcut to the destination, but these nine fundamentals should form the basis of your play. Take the time to read and understand this list and the corresponding tips in the book; then incorporate this knowledge into your game. Doing so will pay off in spades.

1. *Position:* Your location at the table in relation to the betting action will be a key factor in how you play each hand.
2. *Patience:* So easy to understand, so difficult to execute. To win consistently you must depend on skill combined with a little luck, and that takes the patience to wait on the proper starting hands.
3. *Psychology:* Poker is not just about playing the cards you're dealt; it is also about playing the other players.
4. *Changing Gears in Tournament Play:* A good poker player knows when to change his style of play (aggressive versus conservative and coasting, for example). This talent is critical to tournament success.
5. *Making Big Laydowns:* The solid player knows when to fold big hands.
6. *Not Overbetting or Underbetting the Pot in No-Limit:* The biggest single mistake novice no-limit hold'em players make is betting too much or too little. They give no thought to the strategy of the game—when to bet, how much to bet, and why to bet it.
7. *Knowing Your Opponents:* I cannot stress enough how important it is to know how your opponents play. If a very good player, a player you know to be solid, puts in an unusually small raise, he probably wants a call or a reraise. This should be a red flag warning to you—don't cooperate!

8. *Keeping Up with What Cards Are Live or Dead:* You must remember what cards in your hand or on the board could affect the strength of your opponent's hand or the strength of your hand.

9. *Scooping:* In high-low split games your goal is to win the whole pot every time. Never enter the pot with the hope of going only high or only low.

Glossary

Action: The term used for checking, betting, or raising. In a loose game there is a lot of action, which means a lot of betting. The person whose turn it is to bet is said to have the action on him.

Ace-X: An ace with any card lower than a 10 in your hand. For example, A-3.

All In: When a player has put all of his chips into the pot. If a bet, call, or raise takes all the chips in front of a player, he is "all in."

Ante: A required bet from every player at the beginning of a hand. The amount of this forced bet increases at the start of each new level of a tournament. A dealer will often say, "Ante up."

Baby or **Babies**: Small cards, 2, 3, 4, 5, and sometimes a 6.

Baby Pair: Any pair lower than 6s.

Banana: A card that adds no value to your hand. In particular, a high card that hurts a low hand, example: a 9 or above. In poker terminology a banana is synonymous with a "brick."

Best All Round: In some poker tournaments, players receive points for the order in which they finish the tournament. Example: If a tournament has three hundred players, the third player to bite the dust would receive 3 points, the player who placed second place would receive 299 points, the winner would get 300 points, and on down the line. Points from every event are added up and the highest scoring player wins a special prize, often a spiffy new car.

Bicycle: A perfect razz hand; A-2-3-4-5. *See* wheel.

Big Draw: A big potential hand in which you need one card to complete your straight, flush, full house, and so forth.

Big Slick: An ace and a king. A strong starting hand in any hold'em game and even stronger when suited.

Blank: Cards that add no value to a player's hand.

Blind Defender: A player who has a habit of calling raises when he has either the big or the small blind in a hold'em game. This is done to protect his initial investment regardless of the strength of his hand, but it is not good play.

Blinds: A forced bet that one or more players must post in order to start the action on the first round of betting. The blinds rotate clockwise around the table. In most hold'em and Omaha games there are two blinds: the big blind and the small blind.

Bluff: The art of betting or raising with a bad hand and making your opponents think you have the best hand.

Brick: *See* banana.

Brick-and-Mortar: Poker rooms located in a building versus poker played in cyberspace or on the kitchen table.

Bring-In: A mandatory bet by the player dealt the lowest upcard to start the first round of betting in seven-card stud or seven-card stud high-low split. If more than one player has the same rank of low card, then the suits in alphabetical order—clubs, diamonds, hearts, and spades—determine who must start the action. The lowest card in the deck is the deuce of clubs.

Bubble: In a poker tournament, the player who is the last to be eliminated before the prize money is said to be on the "bubble."

Button: A round white disk used to represent the dealer position; also referred to as a dealer button. This marker rotates clockwise around the table for the purpose of indicating from what position the cards are dealt. It also determines who is the first to act.

Bully: A player who repeatedly takes advantage of his intimidation factor and/or chip lead by playing overly aggressive no matter the strength of his hand.

Buy-In: The entry fee for a poker tournament or the amount of chips one purchases for the purpose of playing poker.

Cardroom: The area in a casino where poker is played; also known as the poker room.

Call: The amount of money or chips put into the pot that equals your opponent's bet or raise.

Calling Station: A player who calls all the time with or without a good hand or the potential of making a good hand.

Change Gears: To go from playing tight to loose or playing aggressively to passively or vice versa. This is a very important technique in poker tournaments.

Check: To pass or decline to bet when the action is on you.

Check-Call: To pass or decline to bet when the action is on you but to call if someone behind you bets.

Check-Raise: To pass or decline to bet when the action is on you but to raise if someone behind you bets.

Chip: A token that represents varied denominations of money.

Connectors: Cards that are in consecutive order. Example: 4-5, 8-9, Q-K, and so on. In Omaha you would have four cards 10-J-Q-K or A-2-3-4, and so forth.

Cold-Call: Calling an original bet and a raise.

Counterfeit: To be counterfeited in a poker game is to have the best hand beaten by the cards on the board. Example: You hold a pair of pocket 8s. Your opponent holds Q-A. You have the best hand before the flop. The flop is 9-9-3. You have the best hand after the flop with 8s and 9s. The turn is a jack; you still have the best hand with your two pair. The river card is another jack. You lose to the Q-A because the best hand now is two pair with an ace. The two pair on the board is bigger than your pair. The river card counterfeited your winning hand.

Cut-Off Seat: The position one seat to the right of the button. The button is the best position in a hand of poker. The cut-off seat is the second-best position.

Dealer Button: *See* button.

Deuce: Another way to refer to a 2 card. Example: A 2 of hearts is also called a deuce of hearts.

Door Card: The first upcard in a game of seven-card stud, seven-card stud high-low split, or razz.

Double Through: A term used when you go all in, someone matches your bet, and you win the pot. You have doubled the amount of chips you had.

Drawing Dead: Playing a hand that has no possibility of winning because the cards you need are either in the muck or in the hands of other players. You seldom know that you are drawing dead.

Established Pot: A pot with enough chips in it that it is worth winning at any point.

Felt: The material used to cover poker tabletops. When a player has very few chips, he is said to be down to the felt.

Field: The players in a tournament.

Fifth Street: The third upcard in a hand of seven-card stud, stud high-low, or razz, which is the fifth card in a player's hand.

Fill Up: Making a full house when you have trips, a set, or two pair.

Fish: A weak player, a sucker, a loser. If you can't identify the fish at the poker table, it probably is you.

Flop: The first three community cards in hold'em or Omaha, which are dealt faceup simultaneously.

Flop Game: Any poker game where community cards are used.

Flush: Five cards of the same suit. Example: If you are playing seven-card stud and you are holding a A-J-10-7-2 of hearts, you have an ace-high heart flush.

Fourth Street: The second upcard in a hand of seven-card stud, stud high-low, or razz, which is the fourth card in a player's hand. *See* turn.

Free Card: A card that didn't require calling a bet to see.

Full House: Three of a kind with a pair, such as three kings and two 3s. That is called "kings full of 3s."

Gutshot: A draw to an inside straight, where only one card will complete the hand. Example: J-9-8-7 requires a 10 to complete the straight. For players who go after a gutshot straight, *see* fish.

Heads-Up: A hand in which there are only two players.

Hole: Your first two downcards in seven-card stud, stud high-low, razz, or your downcards in flop games.

Implied Pot Odds: The amount you believe will be in the pot after the betting is done. Often the pot odds will not justify a call, but when the implied odds are considered, a call may be the correct play.

In the Pocket: Your downcards. *See* hole.

Juice: The amount the casino or cardroom takes from the pot for its profit. It usually is 10 percent with a $3 to $5 maximum. Also the amount tacked onto a tournament buy-in to pay expenses.

Kicker: A side card. Not an important card unless you are tied with a player on a hand, then the highest kicker will win. Example: In hold'em, if the board is two pairs and a jack, you will win if you have an ace kicker.

Limit: The amount any player may bet or raise on any round of betting.

Limp In: To enter the pot by calling rather than raising.

Limper: The player who enters the pot for the minimum bet.

Live Card: The cards that are still available and have not yet been seen in any game of poker.

Lone Ace: An ace with another card of no significant value, as in ace-blank or ace-rag.

Loose: Playing more hands than would be considered normal.

Loosey-Goosey: A player who plays almost every hand with no regard to hand value, pot odds, or what another player may be holding.

Muck: The pile of discarded cards in a game of poker.

Multiway Action or **Multiway Pot**: When several players are involved in the same pot.

Move All In: In no-limit when you bet all the chips (money) that you have in front of you in one action.

Make a Move: To try a bluff.

Maniac: A wild, unpredictable player who plays unconventionally and superaggressively with no respect for hand value and no respect for the solid, conservative player.

Nut Flush: The highest possible flush.

Nut-Nut: In Omaha high-low, nut-nut means the best possible high hand and the best possible low hand.

Nut Straight: The highest possible straight.

Nuts: The best possible hand at any given point in a hand of poker.

Offsuit: Not of the same suit. Example: You are holding an ace of hearts and a king of clubs. You have big slick offsuit.

Out-Kicked: When the next highest card determines the winning hand and your card is lower than your opponent's card. Example: In a game of hold'em, if there is a jack on board and you hold Q-J to your opponent's A-J. You both have a pair of jacks, but you are out-kicked, therefore you will lose the pot.

Outs: The possibilities available to make your hand.

Overcard: Any card that is higher than your opponent's card.

Overlay: The amount you can win versus the amount you invest. The more you can win on a small investment, the better the overlay.

Overpair: A pair of high cards in your hand; or in flop games, one in your hand and another on the board. Example: You have a pair of 10s in the pocket in hold'em. The flop brings 9-7-3. You have an overpair.

Paint: Any face card: a king, queen, or jack.

Pass: To check or to fold.

Play Back: Raising or reraising in response to your opponent's bet or raise. Example: You have a bully at your table who always raises when you have the big blind. You pick up a marginal hand and reraise him. You have played back at him.

Play Fast: Aggressively playing one's hand.

Pocket: Another term for your downcards. Example: If you have A-K down, you have big slick in the pocket.

Pocket Pair: A pair in the hole. Example: If you have two 10s down, you have a pocket pair of 10s.

Position: Your location at the table in relation to the betting action.

Pot: The chips in the center of the table.

Pot Committed: If you raise in no-limit and someone reraises you all-in, if you have the majority of your chips already in the pot, you are pot committed.

Pot Odds: Pot odds is the relationship between the current pot to the current bet.

Preflop: Prior to the flop.

Preflop Raise: A raise before the flop.

Quads: Four of a kind.

Rag: A card that is of no value to a player's hand.

Rainbow: A sequence of cards in different suits. Example: If the flop comes 3♠-7♥-Q♣, you have a rainbow flop.

Railbird: Viewers who watch poker competition from the rail, which is actually a rail, a rope, or a half wall surrounding a poker area.

Rake: The amount of money the house (casino, card club, or home game) takes from each poker pot to pay the expenses.

Raise: To bet an additional amount after someone has bet.

Reraise: To raise someone who has raised in front of you.

Ring Game: A game of live poker in a casino or card club. Players can buy in, go broke, and buy in again and play for hours or days. Or they can buy in, play for only a few minutes, and leave the game.

River: The last card dealt in most games.

Rock: An ultraconservative player who plays only premium hands.

Rolled up: In stud games when a player is dealt three of a kind in his first three cards.

Runner: When the next card drawn is the perfect card to fit your hand.

Rush: When a player wins an unlikely number of pots in a relatively short period of time.

Sandbag: To slow-play a hand.

Scare Card: A card that appears to hurt the strength of your hand by making your opponent's hand stronger.

Scoop: In games in which the pot can be won by high and low hands, to scoop the pot is to win both ways, with high and low, simultaneously. This is the object of any high-low game.

Semibluff: To bluff a pot when you have multiple outs, that is, you have the potential to make a winning hand.

Set: Three of a kind.

Short Stack: Having too few chips to make two full bets.

Showdown: The point in a hand of poker on the river when the players show their hands and the pot is awarded to the winner.

Slow-Play: To deliberately check or call with the best hand in hopes of winning more money in the later rounds of betting. Showing no strength while holding a strong hand.

Smooth Call: To call rather than raise an opponent's bet.

Split Pair: A pair with one card up and one card down in seven-card games.

Steal: To aggressively bet with the worst hand with the intention of causing your opponent to fold what is probably the best hand so you can win the pot. To steal a pot is another term for bluffing.

Stiff: A player who never leaves a tip is called a stiff (among other derogatory names).

Straddle or **Live Straddle**: When a player under the gun puts in a raise before the cards are dealt.

Straight: Five consecutive cards of mixed suits. Example: K♠-Q♣-J♦-10♥-9♦. This is a king-high straight.

Structure: The predetermined limits of a game, including antes, blinds, forced bets, subsequent bets, and raises.

Stud: Short for the poker game seven-card stud, in which each player is dealt two downcards, four upcards, and a final downcard. The best five cards out of the seven make your hand.

Suited: Cards of the same suit.

Sweater: A friend or fan who usually sits behind a player or watches from the rail and roots for him to win.

Tell: A habit or mannerism a player possesses that conveys information in direct correlation to the strength or weakness of his hand.

Three Flush: In stud games the first three cards dealt being suited. Example: You are dealt a 3♥-5♥-A♥.

Tight: Playing fewer hands than would be normal.

Top Pair: Having paired the highest card on board in hold'em and having the best pair in stud games.

Tournament: A competition in which poker players vie for cash and prizes.

Trips: Three of a kind.

Turn: The second upcard (fourth street) in stud games or the fourth community card in hold'em.

Two-Outer: When only two cards in the deck can make your hand the winner. Not a good bet.

Under the Gun: The first person to act before the flop in flop games.

Underpair: A small pair to the board. Example: If the flop is K-7-3 and you have an A-3, you have an underpair. *See* overpair.

Wheel: 5, 4, 3, 2, A. A baby straight. Also known as a bicycle.

Win Rate: The amount of money you can or should win in relation to the amount of money you invest.

Wraparound Hand: A hand that can make a straight from either end. Example: K-Q-J-10 can make a straight with a 9 or with an ace.

WSOP: World Series of Poker.

1.
Limit Texas Hold'em

Although no-limit Texas hold'em is growing enormously in popularity (due largely to televised competition), one must have a full understanding of the game of limit hold'em before moving into the arena of no-limit. The basics of both games are the same: the deal, two cards are dealt to each player beginning with the player to the right of the button (see table layout on page 2), followed by a round of betting, the flop, followed by a round of betting, the turn, followed by a round of betting, and last but definitely not least, the river, followed by a round of betting, and then to determine the winner, the showdown. This is where the similarities end. Strategies for limit and no-limit hold'em are totally different! The player who believes that the only difference in these two games is the amount of money you can bet at each betting round has a lot to learn if he wants to become a winning player.

Limit hold'em is much more a game of playing the cards. No-limit hold'em is a game of psychological warfare (playing the people). Not incidentally, position is also a very important factor in either game.

Remember, to be continuously successful at any poker game, one must be continually patient.

Limit Hold'em Tips for the Beginner

1. When you sit down at any poker table, your first order of business is to wait. You want to wait and watch. Try not to play a hand until you have watched eight hands or more. This time of observation will give you an opportunity to get a feel for the table and how the players are playing.

2. Position is so very important. As you can see from the positional tips later on, your position can determine what you play and how you play it.

3. You will make two major decisions before entering a pot. The first big decision you will make is choosing which hands you will play. The second big decision is deciding whether or not to continue playing after you have seen the flop.

4. If you decide you have a good hand to play, see the flop. If the flop is a nice fit to your hand, continue. If it is off in left field compared to your two cards, bid farewell to this hand unless it is checked to you. Always take a free card!

5. Example: You are in middle position holding ace♣-10♦. The flop brings 6♣-5♥-Q♥. That flop missed your hand completely. If it is bet in front of you, let your cards go. On the other hand, if the flop is 10♥-6♣-5♥, you should either bet or raise because you have top pair, top kicker.

6. The flop could also give you a good draw. Say your hand is K♣-10♦. If the flop contains a jack and a queen, you have an open-ended straight draw. Now you want to continue with the hand *if* it is a multiway pot. There is no need to draw at a hand if there are only two other players in the hand or if you are heads up, especially if your opponents are playing aggressively. You are probably drawing while their hands are made.

7. If you have nothing after the flop, fold, save your money, and wait for the next good starting hand. Don't continue a hand on wishes and hopes; it's a very expensive bad habit.

8. If other players at your table play eight or nine hands out of ten, they are not good players. They are there because they want action. Playing properly means nothing to them.

9. One of the attractions about the game of poker is that bad players can win. They can make every decision incorrectly and still win because of the luck factor.

10. As a good player, you will play far fewer hands and occasionally, the yahoo (my slang for bad player) will put a bad beat on you. It hurts and it's aggravating; but you have to look forward, not back. In the long run, at the end of the day or the week, the month, or even the year, the good player will prevail. Eventually the cards will break even and that is when the best player wins.

11. You also need to practice reading the board. Ask yourself, what is the best possible hand? For example, if the board is 2♥-7♥-A♣-10♦-9♥, the nuts (the very best hand possible) is an ace-high heart flush. The second nuts would be a king-high heart flush.

12. The nuts can change from the flop to the turn to the river. Just because you flop a nut hand, it doesn't mean that it will remain the nut hand and you need to bet accordingly.

13. For example, if the flop is 5♥-Q♣-9♣, the nuts at this point would be three queens. If the turn brings the 3♣, now the best hand is an ace-high club flush.

14. However, everything can change on the river if the board pairs the 5. Now the nuts is quad (four) 5s and the second nut is queens full.

15. Hand selection and which position you enter the pot from are very important in limit hold'em. Raising from any position with the top three hands, A-A, K-K, and Q-Q is always a good bet.

16. A-A and K-K are worth a reraise if it has been raised when the action is on you. If you are in late position with A-A and the pot has been raised and reraised when the action gets to you, put in a third bet. At this point you have the nuts and need to play it thusly.

17. Other big hands such as K-A (big slick), J-J, Q-A, or 10-10 need to be played a bit more carefully. If you are playing at a tight table (conservative), raise with these hands from early position. If you are at a loose (aggressive) table, just call from early position—but also call if someone raises from a later position. Finally, if the pot is raised before you, just call.

18. After entering the pot with K-A, J-J, Q-A, or 10-10, the flop, the number of players in the pot, and the action before you will determine what your next action should be. If the flop is all rags (small cards), you should bet if it is checked to you. If the pot has already been opened, you should raise with the J-J or the 10-10.

19. If the turn and the river are not scare cards (a card that appears to make your opponent's hand stronger), then repeat your action unless you were raised on the flop. If that is the case, a check-call is okay.

20. As pretty as K-A or Q-A is, especially from late position, don't fall in love with the hand. Keep in mind that the value of these big hands declines as more players enter the pot.

21. Speaking of big hands, not all three-of-a-kind hands are equal. If you have a pair in the pocket and a third one of your cards appears on the board, you have a set. If the board has a pair that matches one of your cards, you have trips. A set is more powerful than trips—it is more difficult for your opponents to put you on a set.

22. If you flop a beautiful set, hopefully there will be a big card or two also. Your hand is so well disguised that if you're in early position you should go ahead and bet. If you're in late position and the pot is opened before it gets to you, don't raise until the turn when the bet doubles. Maximize the profitability of your set. Anytime you flop a set in hold'em you will win 80 percent of the time!

23. It does not take a nut hand to win a pot. As a matter of fact, it's pretty rare for someone to have the nuts. I know a player who keeps two walnuts in his pocket. At showdown, if he rolls his nuts into the pot, everyone knows he has the nuts. He is a winning player, but he doesn't get to do his "walnut visual" often.

24. Many poker teachers preach, "Take one look at your cards and memorize them; never look back at them." This poker teacher disagrees, especially for the new player. Look at your cards as often as necessary.

25. If you are in a hand until the end, always turn your cards up, even if you think you have a losing hand. Occasionally, you may have been going for one hand, and make another unbeknownst to you.

26. For example, if you were drawing to a flush and missed, but the hand is checked on the river, you may have made a hand you weren't thinking about, like a straight or a baby pair, which could be a winner. Part of the many responsibilities of a dealer is to read all hands that are turned up. If you miss something, he should catch it.

27. Along the same lines, never muck (discard) your cards if someone calls a hand that will beat you until you and/or the dealer sees that hand. Mistakes can be made, and they can be corrected.

28. Example: You start the hand with a pocket pair of jacks. The board is safe (no card over a jack) but there are three hearts. If at the end of the hand your opponent calls out that he has a flush, make sure you see it! He may have the ace of hearts and a 10 of diamonds in his hand. He recalls that he has two red cards and he may believe he made a heart flush. He also may be one of those who listened to the preaching about the command to take only one look at your cards.

29. Always consider your position before entering a pot. Some hands you will fold if you are under the gun (first to act) but you may raise from late position. To reiterate, decisions such as this always depend on the caliber of players at your table.

30. Example: If you are under the gun with a Q-10 offsuit, I recommend you pass (fold). The reason is you might have to call a raise in order to see the flop and you cannot call a double raise. If the flop brings a Q and you bet, what happens if you are raised? How do you like your 10 kicker now?

31. However, if you are on the button (best position) with the same hand and no one has entered the pot, you can consider putting in a raise in hopes of picking up the blinds. Even if you don't and one or both of the blinds call and then check the flop, your bet will probably win you the pot.

32. Continuing with our Q-10 in late position, if a tight player raised in front of you, you should fold. If a loose player raised, you should call and see the flop and then proceed cautiously; if a 10 or a Q comes and the loosey-goosey bets, you should raise!

33. When you are in middle position (see page 2), you can lower your starting hand requirements slightly. In addition to the top-ranked card combinations, you can add hands with lesser value such as A-10, K-10, Q-10, J-10, K-J, Q-J, A-X if suited, and middle pairs (7s, 8s, and 9s).

34. Whether or not you will call a raise with these hands from middle position will depend on who makes the raise. If it is a rock, say good-bye. If it is a loosey-goosey, call the raise and see the flop. If it is a maniac, call the raise and hold your breath!

35. In late position you can really loosen up and call with hands such as small pairs and suited connectors (7-6, 5-4, 8-7, etc.). Enter the pot with this type of weak hand only if the pot has not been raised.

36. The exception to this rule is if a loose player raises from early position and there is multiway action (five or more callers). What this most likely means is that there are a bunch of high cards out so your little ol' 7-6 or 5-4 just might make a straight or two pair. (Careful if you flop one pair and overcards.)

37. Don't make the mistake so many beginners make; you get bored, see an ace, and think—power! One ace is not a powerhouse. It's okay to play any ace suited in late position, but your goal is a nut flush, not an ace! If your small kicker flops, that's okay; but if an ace comes…be careful! You could have kicker problems.

38. To further drive home this point, let's say you are playing at a full table and have an ace-little. You are in late position and all ten players enter the pot. One of the other nine players will have an ace 75 percent of the time. To reiterate, *be careful with that little kicker.*

39. Defending your blinds—don't! Some players are known as blind defenders. This is not good play. If your blind is raised, consider it the price of doing business and don't call with anything less than a pair, an ace with a 10 or higher, or any two paints (face cards). If the raiser is the rock at the table, let it go.

40. On the other hand, if the bully at the table raises your blind every time, you need to play back at him. You can do it with any two cards but I would rather you wait for any pair or medium strength cards (10-9, J-9, K-J, etc.). When he raises your blind again, don't call him—*raise* him. He may call to see the flop. You should bet the flop no matter what it is. If the flop didn't hit his hand, he will be gone and you will have the satisfaction not only of winning the pot, but also of punching the bully.

41. If you play in brick-and-mortar poker rooms you eventually will encounter a play called a *live straddle*. This happens when a player under the gun puts in a raise before the cards are dealt. Usually a player who will make this bet wants a lot of action, feels invincible, is trying to intimidate everyone, or is intoxicated.

42. In my professional opinion, anyone who would make a live straddle raise is an idiot. As a player, do not get involved in such a pot without a strong hand with which you can reraise.

43. Another poker oddity you may encounter is a *kill game*. A kill game usually doubles the blinds if one player wins two pots in a row. There are also half-kill games.

44. Example: If you are playing a $5-$10 game and the same player wins two pots in a row, he is forced to make a blind bet of $20 and the blinds for the next hand become $10-$20. The game literally goes from $5-$10 to $10-$20. If the same player wins a third time, it remains the kill limit. If you find yourself in a half kill game of $10-$20 and win two pots in a row, your blinds will then go up to $15-$30 rather than a full kill of $20-$40.

45. You can find kill games both in brick-and-mortar poker rooms and Internet poker rooms. If you are not comfortable with them, do not take a seat in a kill game. If you like the idea of the higher limit in the lower-limit game, just to mix it up a bit, your seat is waiting.

46. Occasionally when you are in the big or small blind all the other players at the table will fold, leaving only you and the big blind. If you both agree, you can "chop" and each take back your blind bet. Some players chop; others never chop. It is a personal decision. However, establish up front whether or not your tablemate will chop. If you agree to chop one time, you should do it every time during the session.

47. Check-raising is often considered rather rude in a home game, but in real poker games it is a powerful tool. Check-raising is a method used to get more money in the pot when you have a powerhouse of a hand.

48. Bluffing and semibluffing in low-limit games are usually exercises in futility. You must be playing against very good players in order to have a bluff respected, so save this strategy for when you step up to intermediate play and higher limits.

49. Remember: When playing ring games or tournament poker, it isn't how many pots you play, it's how many pots you win! Speaking of poker tournaments…

50. Poker tournaments are fun and offer great overlays. As a beginner, play only low buy-in tournaments until you believe that you are ready to graduate to higher-limit buy-in tournaments.

51. A great place to practice poker tournaments is on the Internet. (See chapter 11.)

52. Most brick-and-mortar poker rooms offer daily poker tournaments ranging in price from $5 up to top of the line at the Bellagio in Las Vegas where the price tag is a hefty $1,000 plus the $60 juice (the money the casino takes for the house). You can often see poker superstars honing their skills there.

53. All tournaments will have the juice built in for the house. It will start at $1 and go higher, depending on the event. This money goes to pay the casino's expenses for hosting the tournament.

54. The smaller buy-in tournaments are so popular that they will often sell out. If you have your heart set on participating, I suggest you arrive at least an hour early to sign up. You can also call the casino and ask them if they expect to sell out and if so, how early you should arrive to assure yourself a seat. Some casinos will allow you to make a phone reservation for a tournament seat.

55. The basics of a poker tournament are as follows: you show up, sign up, and pay up. You then take a seat, usually chosen at random.

56. You will start with low-limit blinds, usually $5-$10 and play this level for fifteen or twenty minutes after which the blinds will increase, probably to $10-$20.

57. The blinds will continue to increase and you will have a potty break every couple of hours. If you are in a rebuy tournament (if you go broke you can rebuy and get more chips), the rebuys will end after a designated amount of time, usually the first hour, which equates to the first three or four rounds.

58. If you are in a rebuy tourney, decide before the event how many rebuys you will allow yourself and then play accordingly. Personally, I prefer a tournament with no rebuys; that way no one can have an advantage.

59. A poker tournament is a process of elimination. When a player loses all of his money, he leaves the table. The last soldiers left standing win the money.

60. The payout for a tournament depends on how many players enter the competition and the pay structure of that particular casino. There is no absolute standard but first place usually receives 35 to 40 percent of the prize pool and they normally pay one place for every ten players (for example, the top twenty-five places will be paid in a tournament with two hundred fifty entrants).

61. Playing a poker tournament is exactly like playing a regular game in the early stages of the tournament. You should play a conservative game and observe your opponents while paying close attention to your position.

62. After the early stages (the first two or three rounds) everything changes. I mentioned earlier how vastly differently the games limit and no-limit hold'em are. The same holds true for the differences in a ring game and a poker tournament.

63. There are four stages to a poker tournament: the early stages, the middle stages, the late stages, and the final table. (Yippee! The final is your goal.)

64. As mentioned, in the early stages, play very carefully and study your opponents. Knowing how your opponents play provides valuable information for later in the tournament.

65. Remember this: You cannot win a poker tournament in the first three rounds of play, but you sure as heck can lose it. There is no need to play fast and aggressively early on.

66. In the middle stages of the tournament, you will need to change gears. During these levels many players will be eliminated. You will have to start playing more hands, always keeping in mind your position and how your opponents are playing.

67. If you are short-stacked during the late stages of the tournament, you're going to have to pick a hand and make a move. The shorter your stack, the lower your starting hand requirements.

68. Try not to blind yourself out of a tournament. If your cards are cold and you just can't seem to pick up a decent starting hand, wait for the right time and try to have enough money in late position to raise the pot. Choose a time when no one has entered the pot and raise with almost any two cards, suited is better or connected (8-7 or 10-6 of the same suit and so forth).

69. Do not limp in a pot with a short stack. If you go down, go down swinging!

70. On the other hand, if you have a big stack, raise and try to steal the blinds as often as the other players will let you. Lower your starting hand requirements if a short stack raises the pot. He is probably desperate and any ace or any two paints is worth a call or a reraise if that will put him all in.

71. If you have a medium stack, play cautiously but be aggressive at certain times. As my friend Professor Tom McEvoy advises, "Play selectively aggressive." (This also is very good advice for ring games.)

72. When you arrive at the final table, how you play will depend on your goals. If you will not be happy with anything less than first place, you're going to have to be superaggressive and gamble more in an effort to get all the chips.

73. If your goal as a new player is simply to step up in the pay table as much as you can, you will play accordingly, laying down playable hands if there are many short stacks being gobbled up by the monster stacks. Every player who is eliminated means a larger payday for you!

74. Remember two things about tournament play. No one ever won a poker tournament without getting lucky more than once! And remember the old adage, all you need is a chip, a chair, and a prayer.

75. Poker is not an exact science. If it were, the good players would always win and the bad players would always lose, then quit and there goes our fish! There are many variables to each and every hand.

Limit Hold'em Tips for the Intermediate Player

76. When you go out or have people in your home to play poker, what is your goal? Most would answer to win or to make money. That answer is ultimately correct but your primary goal should be to make the right decisions because if you make the correct decisions in poker, you will, in the long run, win money.

77. If you're reading the intermediate tips, you have probably been playing limit hold'em for a while and have confidence that you know the ins and outs of the game.

78. But are you a winning player? Do you play for fun or profit? Do you keep records? Do you know whether you're a winning or a losing player, overall? If you don't know, you should.

79. If you do not keep records and you want to play poker for profit, now is the time to start. Buy a pocket calendar and keep an honest account of your wins and losses. Don't be like the horseplayer who came home from the track and told his wife, "I won $1,600!" What he failed to tell her was that his total output on bets that day was $1,550, so his net win was only $50.

80. Your records can be as simple or as detailed as you want. You can track where you play, what days you play, and what time of day you play in addition to your net for each session.

81. You may discover after a month of record keeping that you play your best between 10 a.m. and 3 p.m. or after dinner, at a certain poker room, and that you seem to win more on certain days of the week. The most important information you need to record is that of your wins and losses.

82. If you play both live and on the Internet, keep two sets of records. You can add them together at the end of the year for a grand total, but you need to know where and when you are winning the most money. Ultimately, this is where you will want to invest most of your poker time, money, and energy.

83. If you believe you just aren't disciplined enough to keep records, then I believe that you aren't disciplined enough to be a winning poker player—so there! Remember, as you study your records, the end of a session isn't what you're concerned with, or even the end of a week or a month. The bottom line is the end of the year.

84. Your goal, of course, is to have a winning session every time you play, but let's get real—that isn't going to happen. Anyone who tells you that he wins every time he plays is either a liar or he played twice in his life, booked two wins, and retired from the poker arena forever.

85. A winning poker player does not play a lot of hands unless he is on a rush. A good poker player will recognize a rush, play it for all it's worth, but also recognize when it is over.

86. You know what your starting hand requirements are and from what position they should be played. When you have a long dry spell and have seen nothing but 7-2, 8-3, K-7 for hours, you can do three things: play anything from late position because you are bored (I do not recommend this strategy), go home and come back another day, or continue to be patient. The cards will turn.

87. On some days, after that dry spell and when the cards do turn, you may find that your good cards are getting squished. If that is the case, you're running bad. Now you still have three things you can do: beat your head against the wall, pull out more money to invest in the game (I do not recommend either of these), or go home and come back another day—this is the best solution.

88. After an hour or so into a session, your tablemates, if they are paying attention as you have, will have you pegged as a solid player, maybe even conservative. Now is the time for a bluff or two.

89. If you're in a $10-$20 game, the blinds are probably $5 and $10, or in a $15-$30, they are likely $10 and $15. That is costing you $15 or $35 a round. Every now and then when you are on the button or in the cutoff seat (the position one seat to the right of the button), you will need to raise on a bluff or a semibluff just to try to pick up the blinds.

90. After some time at the table you should have a feeling of how your opponents are playing. You will know if you are playing against blind defenders or not. So take a stab at it with a cold bluff or a semibluff.

91. Before doing so from the cutoff seat, try to have a read on the player on the button. If a player is going to fold, many times you can tell by his body language. Often, that language practically screams, "I am going to fold," because he is holding his cards in a "muck position."

92. If you have had a long dry spell, try raising on a bluff or a semibluff with any ace or maybe even any king or queen. Even if you have a blind defender, your high card might be the best hand or you could catch a good flop.

93. However, if you don't get a good flop and the blind check-raises you or calls your bet, simply check the turn; or if he bets, abandon ship and wait for another opportunity. Cut your losses.

94. Once you decide to play a hand after the flop, you should become the aggressor even from early position. Consider this: if you know you will call a bet, why not take the lead and bet in the first place? Checking is a sign of weakness; betting or raising is a sign of strength.

95. This move helps you determine your opponent's strength. You can't determine the strength of anyone else's hand by checking.

96. Example: You are in the big blind with a K♥-3♥. The flop is A♥-7♥-3♣. You know you will call a bet, so why not bet it? Even if your opponents call, you might make a huge hand if another heart comes. If your bet is raised, you may be facing an ace, but your bet has gained information for you. You then can decide whether or not you want to proceed with this hand.

97. If it is a multiway pot, I would continue on that great big beautiful heart flush hunt. However, if it is heads up and someone raised, I'd not gamble on this one. The odds are not in your favor.

98. If you have a marginal hand that you bet in late position on both the flop and the turn, do not bet it again on the river. Ask yourself these two questions, "If he calls, will I lose?" and "If he raises, can I call? " If the answer is yes to the first question and no to the second, then just check.

99. Take advantage of tight players in the blind and raise often from late position. However, don't do it every time—you will lose your credibility.

100. Don't even think about bluffing a calling station (one who calls bets all the time with or without a good hand or the potential for a good hand) or inexperienced players who are playing higher limit games because they can. I was in a $15-$30 game one time when a bad player made a bad call on the turn and caught his two-outer (only two cards in the deck that can make the hand a winner) on the river. His opponent snarled, "How could you make that call on the turn?" To which the inexperienced player replied, "Because I'm rich!"

101. The time to semibluff is when your hand probably is not strong enough to win the pot on the flop but could improve by the turn or the river. This means you have outs. If you bet, the other players may fold, they may give you a free card on the turn, or—in a perfect scenario— you may actually make the hand you have been representing.

102. Some examples of semibluffing: You are holding the A♦-4♦. The flop brings J♦-4♣-6♦. You have flopped bottom pair and the nut-flush draw. If there is four-way action, you are in late position, and it is bet, raise it. If it is checked, bet it. If you are in early to middle position, bet it.

103. Most semibluff situations arise when you have a straight or a flush draw. Another example: You are holding the J♦-10♣. The flop is K♣-Q♠-3♥. You have an open-end straight draw; unless there is a lot of raising and reraising in front of you, go for the semibluff.

104. Be aware that other good players will also be bluffing and semibluffing. If you believe that is the case, act accordingly. Remember to give even less credibility to a bully. There is nothing sweeter (besides maybe winning a major tournament) than having the table bully feeling completely confident in his efforts to run over the table until you pick up a big hand and trap the pest.

105. Even without a big hand, if you have a bully at the table and he is on the button when you have the big blind, he probably is stealing from you far too often. Now is the time to defend your big blind with a marginal hand (two paints, a small pair, or ace-X). Defend with a reraise. He will probably fold, but if he doesn't, then either bet the flop or check-raise.

106. If you are on a drawing hand, a straight, or a flush, you want more players in the pot to make it worthwhile to invest in your draw. This comes under the heading of pot odds and outs, which will be discussed in the section for advanced players.

107. On the other hand, if you have top pair, you want to try to limit the number of players. If you don't try to limit the players, one of them may be on a draw and make it.

108. Big pairs hold up much better with fewer players in the pot. Heads-up is preferable.

109. Generally, play a conservative and controlled game but on occasion mix up your play. You don't want to be predictable. Good players will notice and hesitate when trying to read how you play.

110. Example: Play big pairs in early position with a raise 75 percent of the time. Just call the other 25 percent. But if somebody in late position raises, jump back at him with a reraise.

111. The 1995 World Poker Champion, Dan Harrington, has a terrific formula for knowing when to raise with a big pair and when to just call. This formula is based on raising 80 percent of the time. Look at your watch. Since 80 percent of 60 is 48, if the second hand is between 0 and 48, raise. If it is between 48 and 60, just call. You can read more in his book *Harrington on Hold'em.*

112. Playing overcards can be costly if you don't hit on the flop. Players who check and call with overcards to smaller cards on the board are not winning players.

113. If one of your overcards does hit on the flop, good for you, unless there is a straight or a flush possibility—then you shouldn't like it so much. Tread lightly.

114. A tight player who begins to play overly aggressive should set off an alarm in your head. Remember, a baby set will crush your big strong overpair (a pair of high cards either in your hand or one in your hand and one on the board).

115. Ace-king and ace-queen are over-rated. Many people will play these cards as if they are aces, kings, or queens. The fact of the matter is a baby pair can beat them.

116. If you have big slick and raise from any position, be careful if you don't catch either of your cards on the flop, especially if a rock is staying with you. If that is the case, I would check, and if he bets, fold.

117. If you are in early position with A-K against just one or two players, bet the flop to gain information. If you are raised, fold. If you are called and don't catch on the turn, check.

118. Keep in mind that ace-king and ace-queen are just two big cards unless you pair. You will hit that pair about 29 percent of the time.

119. Get all the money in the pot you can with your big hands. There will be times you don't want to run the other players off.

120. Example: You are holding K♠-J♥. The flop is K♥-J♣-7♦. You have flopped the top two pair. If there was no preflop raise, you should feel very confident with this hand, so either check-call from early position against one player, saving the check-raise for the turn when the bet doubles, or check-raise if it is a multiway pot. If it is bet or raised before you, you should reraise.

121. There is always an exception in every hand of poker. Using the above example, the rule would be: If a rock is swinging hard punches, beware of a set of 7s. In other words, anytime an extremely tight player is playing overly aggressive, beware of him having a set or any hand that can beat you. Play back at him *only if you have the nuts.*

122. If you flop the bottom two pair, you probably have a good hand unless there is a straight or a flush possibility. Bet accordingly.

123. Example: You are in late position with 9♦-8♦. The flop is A♦-9♠-8♣. If someone bets, raise. If they check, bet. If there is an ace-rag or an ace-big against you, you don't want him drawing to his kicker nor do you want someone drawing to a straight.

124. If you have a straight draw or a flush draw and make your hand on the turn, good for you, bet accordingly. However, if the board pairs, beware!

125. Anytime the board pairs you must consider the possibility that someone else has a full house. They even could have quads. Your hand just went from "yippee, I've got the nuts" to "proceed with caution."

126. Most of the time you will call a bet in front of you if you were going to bet it anyway. That does not mean you would call a raise. It depends on who makes the raise and the strength of your hand.

127. There is a win-rate formula that a good hold'em player should win at least one big bet an hour. If you're playing $5-$10, that isn't a decent wage, so I hope you're just playing for fun. If you're playing $30-$60, $60 an hour isn't too shabby, depending on how many hours you are able to play.

128. If you want to make the big bucks for your limit hold'em efforts for an investment of $50, $100, $500, or more, tournament poker is the way to go. So now for some tournament tips.

129. It takes money to make money in the real world or in the poker world. However, the overlay in poker tournaments (major or minor) can be breathtaking—even life changing. With some skill, some luck, lots of stamina, and patience, you too can learn to score in poker tournaments.

130. If you believe that the way to win a major poker tournament is to play the way you have seen the finalists play on TV, you couldn't be more wrong. Keep in mind that the TV poker contests you watch began the competition days earlier with hundreds, if not thousands, of entrants.

131. They have played anywhere from twenty-four to forty hours over a period of days to arrive at that coveted final table. During those tedious hours of competing, the strategy of play has metamorphosed over and over again. This is called *changing gears* and is one of the biggest differences in ring games and tournament play.

132. During those three or four days of play, they have survived through fifteen to twenty rounds of play. The rounds last anywhere from one to two hours and the blinds increase with each round.

133. If you believe that if you are a good limit hold'em player you will automatically be a good hold'em tournament player, you are way off base. Becoming a winning tournament player requires a strategy all its own.

134. After studying the following tips and giving tournament competition a try, you will probably love it or hate it. You must have stamina, patience, guts, and heart to compete properly in tournaments. The strategies I am going to share with you can be used in small buy-in tourneys or huge ones.

135. I can't say enough about having patience in a poker tournament. You cannot win a tournament in the beginning stages, but you sure as heck can lose it! The first two or three rounds are the time to wait for only good starting hands and watch your opponents. Study them and play very few hands. The hands you select to play should be big hands, which you should win; however, if you lose them, never, ever give up.

136. Your goal for the beginning stages of the tournament is to win a few hands per level and study your opponents. Now you are ready for the middle stages, which include rounds five through eight.

137. The field begins to narrow in the middle stage of a tournament. You should change gears and begin to play more hands.

138. The limits are higher and it is now worth a slight risk to get the blinds from the middle of the table to your slowly building empire, especially if you can pick up another bet or two along with them. If you know a player has been doing a lot of limping to see the flop but will fold if the pot is raised, you should raise and try to steal the blinds and the limper's bet at the right time when you are in late position.

139. After the flop you will know what the nuts or second nuts can be. There will be times to represent a hand that you do not have.

140. For example, you are holding an A♦-10♣. The flop brings three diamonds. The nuts is an ace-high diamond flush. You do not have that hand but you can sure represent it. You have that beautiful ace of diamonds, therefore nobody else can have the nuts. If a loosey-goosey bets, raise to slow him down and give yourself an inexpensive opportunity to make your nut flush or catch an ace for top pair. If a rock bets, raise; he may fold even if he has a flush. Now is the time to play your players as well as your holdings.

141. The poor to average players will play basically the same way as they go through a tournament until they are eliminated. As they are eliminated—and many will be in the middle stages because their chips will be finding a new home in your chip stack—new players will take their seats or your table will break as the tournament directors fill empty seats. When this happens, change gears again and go back to the early stage strategy until you familiarize yourself with your new opponents.

142. When you believe you have them pegged, play them accordingly. For example, in limit hold'em don't go up against the table maniac unless you have a powerhouse, and then let him self-destruct.

143. If you're first to act and flop two pair or better, and you know your opponent will bet into any check, you should check-call. Don't raise until the bet doubles on the turn. If he is first to act and bets into you and you believe you have the best of it, don't raise because you don't want to lose him. Maximize your big opportunities.

144. Realistically, you don't have to win a lot of hands as you proceed through the middle stages because the pots are getting bigger and bigger with every level increase. The secret is winning your fair share and not losing pots or getting involved in hands that could ultimately cost you a big portion of your hard-earned chips.

145. Know when to get away from a hand and know how to make the most of a monster hand. Sadly, there will be times when the best play is to lay down a monster hand.

146. Example: You have two beautiful aces. It was called from two positions and raised from middle position. You, of course, will reraise because you want to get it heads-up and that is exactly what happens.

147. So far so good, everything is going according to plan. But wait! The flop comes Q-Q-7. If he check-raises you or even check-calls, a big red flag should go up. If he is a solid player, he knows you have a big hand because of your preflop reraise, and he is hanging around with a big hand. Now is the time—it is so difficult—but you must fold. This is called *making a big laydown.* It takes an excellent player to be able to do this.

148. The famous granddaddy of all poker greats, Doyle Brunson, tells a story of laying down pocket kings preflop in a major tournament. The reason? He had just won a huge pot and knew that his stack of chips could take him far in the tournament. If he called what was a hefty bet and lost, he would be struggling to rebuild. Rather than take the chance of losing to an ace, he made the difficult decision to fold his kings. (Good move. Are you a poker *player?* Could you do the same?)

149. When you enter the late stages of a tournament you will be among the remaining 20 to 25 percent of the original field. Players will be dropping like flies and you will almost smell the money because you will be getting close to a payday. You had to play well to get to this point, so stay focused.

150. Late in a tourney, when players are focusing on making the money, many will tighten up their play. This is a good opportunity to pick up the blinds (which will be huge by now).

151. Do your best to avoid a confrontation with another big stack but it is okay to go against a short stack, even with a marginal hand. Never ever leave a short stack with even one chip in front of him. If you have a playable hand, put him all in. Even if a short stack draws out on you, he cannot hurt you too badly, and if all goes well, you will eliminate him and be one step closer to the money.

152. If you are in middle-chip position late in a tourney, wait for a good hand but try to steal the antes or blinds at least once a round just to stay even. If you are at a conservative table you may be able to steal more.

153. If you find yourself short-stacked, don't panic, just change gears. Your starting hand requirements must be lowered.

154. If you survive the late stages of the tournament, good for you! You are either in the money or very near the money. Stay focused, be patient, and bluff when you can.

155. If you are the short stack at your final table, you are going to need to take a stand soon. However, if there is another short stack that will be hit with their blinds before you, wait. If they go belly up, you'll move up a notch in the standings. In a major tournament this could mean thousands of dollars.

156. If you start final table play in medium chip position, wait for decent starting hands unless a short stack makes his stand and you have average cards. Remember, he is desperate so it is worth your risk and he cannot bust you.

157. Do your best to stay away from the big stacks. They can bust you. You must be selective about who you will go up against.

158. As the final table field is eliminated, everyone will appear to be playing faster because fewer players are dealt in and each hand takes less time to play. If you're staying focused, playing by the book (this book!), and getting lucky, you just might find yourself heads-up!

159. When you get to heads-up play you cannot show weakness. You will have to defend your blinds with almost any two cards. After all, any two cards can flop. I have won many more heads-up competitions flopping good to a bad hand than trapping with a good hand.

160. Vary your play but retain the aggressive, unafraid attitude. Limp often enough so that when you have a monster hand you can limp without making your opponent overly suspicious.

161. After you win, don't forget to tip the dealers—2.5 percent to 5 percent of your winnings is considered reasonable. All establishments take juice and some pay the dealers a percentage of the juice. It is okay to ask what percentage if any the dealers have already gotten and then do the math. Be sure to deduct your buy-in and then calculate how much the proper tip would be. If you are a generous person, 10 percent would be considered Christmas for the dealers! Any more and they go home talking about you and blessing you.

162. Good energy from a bunch of happy dealers never hurt anybody! There are many dealers who root (on the inside) for certain players to win a tournament because those players are so generous. Other players get reverse sweat (negative energy) from the dealers because they are stiffs (never leave a tip).

163. Whatever you decide to tip is divided among dealers and floorpeople who worked your tournament. If there is a special dealer or two who seemed to deal you winners over and over, it is okay to seek them out and press a little something extra into their palm. Do so discreetly. This also is a nice gesture to any floorpeople who have gone out of their way to be nice to you.

164. So you're the advanced player. You're the best in your home poker club? You're the best poker player in your hometown? You're so good you're about ready to turn pro? Here's the best tip I will be giving you in the entirety of this book: DON'T!

165. I have seen it happen over and over again. The best hometown poker player decides to take a shot at the big leagues. He moves to Las Vegas with his pocket bulging with his life savings. In a year or so, he is busted and disgusted.

166. Absolutely come to Las Vegas for the experience. Have a wonderful poker-filled visit and then go home if that is where you win continually. Keep in mind that the best poker players in the world are in Las Vegas.

167. Come, if you must, with your savings and stars in your eyes but—and here is the second best tip I am going to give you—get a real job in addition to chasing that green-felt dream. At the very least, get a real part-time job, just in case of emergencies—like bad luck causing you to go belly up at the poker table.

168. Whether you're chasing a dream in Las Vegas or beating your home games, you absolutely must have good money management. And you must have some money to manage, hence the job.

169. I advocate a stop-loss on your wins as well as your losses. If you're on a good win, say $900 in a $15-$30 game, put a stop-loss at about $750. Seventy-five percent of your win is a good measure to go by, or get as close as you can come.

170. In other words, if you're sitting on a $1,000 win and get involved in a monster pot that you lose on the river—along with $400 of your winnings—go home! If you chase a bigger win, you could get up a small loser rather than a big winner.

171. Have a stop-loss on any losses that you are comfortable with but be reasonable. Don't put yourself in a position of losing so much that it would take three winning sessions to make it up. A good rule of thumb is to put your stop-loss at approximately what you might expect to make up in one session.

172. Many top pros are former mathematicians, accountants, and CPAs, while some actually have a photographic memory. As we discuss pot odds, outs, and implied pot odds, you will understand why.

173. The poker player who understands pot odds and implied pot odds will have a definite advantage at the poker table. *Pot odds* refer to the relationship between the current pot and the current bet. *Implied pot odds* are your best guess as to what will be in the pot when the betting is finished. Often the pot odds will not justify a call, but when the implied pot odds are considered, a call may be the correct play.

174. In order to calculate your pot odds, you need to determine (your best guesstimate) the number of "outs" you have (the number of cards left in the deck that will make your hand a winning hand). The payoff if you win the pot compared to the odds against you winning determines if it is a good bet.

175. Simplistically, the fewer outs you have, the bigger the pot has to be in order for you to call a bet. The more outs you have, the easier it gets to call a bet. In other words, how much is in the pot and how much may be in the pot when the betting is done (implied pot odds) versus how much it will cost you to play should determine your next moves.

176. Example: Let's say you flop a nut-flush draw. There are thirteen cards of each suit. You have two and there are two on the board. I always guesstimate that two more of my suit are in other player's hands or in the muck, so that leaves seven cards in the deck that will make your hand. Divide seven into the cards remaining in the deck (forty-five) to get 6.4. This means that it is 6 to 1 against you making your hand. To have the pot odds you need, the pot needs to be six times (or more) what it will cost you to call a bet and try to make your hand. (This guesstimate includes your implied pot odds.)

177. To complicate things a bit further, if you are holding an ace and you believe that if an ace comes it also will give you the winning hand, you can add three more cards to your calculations. Now there are ten cards (instead of just seven) that will make your hand. Divide ten into the remaining forty-two cards and your odds are closer to 4-to-1. That's better.

178. Many professional players do the math (in an instant) and know whether they have good pot odds. They are analytical players.

179. Other players, myself included, look at our approximate outs versus the size of the pot versus what we think the players yet to act will do, and then decide if we believe we should gamble and try to make our hand. We are called intuitive players.

180. We, who are not human calculators, use our intuition or our best guess to determine if a call is worth the risk. It's quite simple, actually. Just ask yourself if the pot is big and if it will get bigger versus how much investment it will take to draw to your hand. Then make the decision on whether or not to gamble on the next card.

181. There are two reasons to raise before the flop: to get more money in the pot because you think you have the best hand, or to narrow the field. If the pot has been raised when you are trying to narrow the field so your big pair or big slick will hold up, reraise.

182. There are three reasons to raise after the flop: to bluff because you don't think anybody made a hand, to get a free card, or to gain information. If you believe you still have the best hand after the flop, you again will want to raise or reraise.

183. On the opposite end of that spectrum is the concept of slow-playing. Some hands are just too big to bet. It's a smart move to play a strong hand weakly to keep as many players in the pot as possible, thus building the pot.

184. Your goal with slow-playing, in addition to building the pot, is to give your opponent the opportunity to make a big hand also. If you have the nuts and he has the second nuts—beautiful! Mission accomplished. Your pot will be huge.

185. As an advanced player, bluffing should be in your repertoire, but use it sparingly. Anyone who raises too many pots is labeled a bully. You want to set yourself up as a solid player so that your bluffs will be respected.

186. The most successful bluffs or semi-bluffs are those made by solid players. The reason is that the majority of the times that there is a showdown, the solid player shows a winning hand, so other players expect it of him. Therefore, when he does bluff or semibluff another good player, that player will have to have a big hand to call.

187. Never forget: you cannot bluff a bad player. They just don't get it. Save your bluffs for the more sophisticated opponent.

188. My personal favorite is the semi-bluff. You may win the pot then and there or you may get action and then improve your hand to become the legitimate winner.

189. I especially like to semibluff from the big blind if there is a bully on the button. Usually you can win it before the flop.

190. Bad beats and bad luck are often synonymous. An advanced poker player must take his beats like a man—not a cry-baby, a real man (or woman!).

191. I'm not saying you need to pat the table and say, "Nice hand," to some knucklehead who just played a two-outer against your pocket kings and made it. I am saying don't fuss and cuss and stew over it. This will hurt no one but you, and frankly, no one wants to hear it.

192. An old joke in the poker world goes like this:

Q: Do you know the difference between a puppy and a losing poker player?

A: The puppy will eventually stop whining!

193. An advanced player knows how to let it go almost immediately and look forward, not back. The good part is that the knucklehead will continue to play badly, so look at your loss simply as an investment, which he is holding and will return to you with great interest.

194. The fact is, hold'em is more than just a card game. Whenever you're dealing with people, you are dealing with psychological influences. Not only theirs but also yours.

195. You must have terrific control over your emotions, not only to play your best game but also so as not to give off any tells. If you think you have lost that control, then it's time to stop and play another day, or at the very least take a walk and cool down.

196. Just as a bad player can get lucky, a good player can get unlucky. As a good player, you should always have a positive expectation when you enter a game. However, if you have been playing poker regularly for a year or more, you have experienced one of those horrid freaks of poker nature called a losing streak. It can wreak psychological havoc on even the best of players.

197. The solution: take a good, long look at your game. Have you changed anything? Are you trying to make something good happen by playing too many hands? You know that isn't going to work. Take a break, a long break, and every time you start a new game, play your best. Eventually it will stop, I promise—as long as you're doing your part by playing your A-game all the time.

198. As Bill Burton, poker player extraordinaire and poker author, says, "Luck comes and goes. Knowledge stays forever." Bad players depend on luck; you can depend on your knowledge.

199. The flip side of that coin is that you too will get lucky and beat the best hand many times in your poker career. The adage in tournament poker is that if you win an event, you will have gotten lucky at least five times; the longer the competition, the more times you will have gotten lucky. You must combine this with good play. Poker tournament expert Tom McEvoy says, "You must be a skillful poker player in tournaments in order to put yourself in a position to get lucky."

200. Know your opponents but don't let them know you. Study their play, have a feel for what they are doing and why. However, don't let them figure you out. Play a solid game, but not a predictable one. Mix your play up just enough to keep them guessing.

201. Example: Don't always raise with your big hands up front. Don't always reraise with them in late position. Call a raise occasionally with suited connectors. Surprise them with your holdings. Don't be predictable.

202. Play in your comfort zone. If you were a winning $10-$20 player who stepped up to a $15-$30 limit and did well for a couple months, you might decide to go up another level to $20-$40. Let's say at that level things changed for you and you stopped winning. Whatever the reason, if you are not comfortable in one level, don't be embarrassed to step back down. You want to play where you win the most. For some that is $15-$30; for others it may be $100-$200. It's your money and your choice.

203. Some good players believe that the higher the level they can afford to play, the more money they can win. That isn't always true. If you win more pots in $10-$20 versus winning approximately an equal number of pots in $30-$60 but you also are losing more, you have accomplished an investment reversal.

204. Don't call on the river when your gut says no. Have the discipline to make those difficult laydowns. Listen to yourself.

205. Example: You hold A♥-A♣. Of course that is the perfect starting hand, but not always the perfect ending hand. You raise from middle position. A calling station calls you plus you get a call from the big blind. The flop comes 10♥-J♠-3♠. The big blind checks. You bet and both of them call. The turn is A♠. (You have a beautiful set, but did that ace make a straight for someone or a spade flush?) The big blind checks. You bet and the calling station raises. Could he have a K-Q? Of course he could even though you don't want him to, and to make matters worse, the blind calls his raise. You need to fill up or move out. The river is the 7♠. The big blind checks. You check. The calling station bets. The big blind raises. Now what? This one isn't even a difficult decision. In all likelihood you are up against a straight and a flush! At the very least *one* of them has your set of aces beat. Time to make a big laydown.

206. Another example: You are holding K♠-Q♠ and the flop brings K♥-Q-♥-3♥. Initially I would like this hand…but wait. You are in late position, thinking about those chips coming to you when there is a bet and a raise before the action gets to you. There certainly can be a flush out there, a flush draw, a straight draw, or a set to beat you.

207. Whether or not you pay the price to see the turn will depend on who bet. If it is a rock betting or raising, I would not. However, if the player betting or raising would do so on the come, then give it a call. If the turn is a heart or a 10, you should fold to any bet; if it is a blank the same advice holds true for the river. Sometimes you have to tiptoe through the minefield.

208. The movie star Mimi Rogers is a poker player. She once told me that the hardest poker lesson she ever learned was that your aces and kings can be beaten. "Always think about that set that could be out there," she said. "I learned the hard way!"

209. Now let's talk about the limit hold'em game played in poker tournaments. Go back to the intermediate, even the beginner tips for tournament play and then we'll add a few advanced plays for your portfolio.

210. Into the later rounds of the tournament, your chip count will determine what gear you need to shift to. As you near the money, you should constantly be aware not only of your chip count but also that of your opponents, including those at the other remaining tables.

211. At these levels the antes and blinds are going to be so expensive that you won't have the luxury of waiting for those premium hands unless you have a substantial chip lead. You're going to have to pick various favorable spots and then hold your breath and jump in.

212. You will see many lucky flops or lucky drawouts during a tournament, especially in the later stages. This is part of the game. You too will be making some of these lucky draws (hopefully).

213. Most major tournaments will have a viewable time clock to let you know how much time is left in each round. This is very important information.

214. If there is not a time clock in your line of view, have one with you. You can get small timers at any store that carries small appliances or kitchen aids.

215. Watch the time, especially if your chips are dwindling. You will want to make a move before a structure increase.

216. Let's say you are playing $3,000-$6,000. You have $25,000 in front of you. The next level will be $4,000-$8,000. With your $25,000, a preflop raise at the $3,000-$6,000 limit will leave you with $19,000 to work with after the flop. If you wait and the next level increase comes into effect, your preflop raise to $16,000 leaves you only with $9,000 after the flop. It is much more likely that you will be called. Make your move early when your chips can still be threatening.

217. When you get to heads-up (congratulations!) you cannot be the least bit passive. You must take the lead with aggression. Any paint or ace is worth a preflop raise or reraise.

218. However, do not raise every time. Do mix in a call now and then. That way, when you pick up a big pair or big slick, you can have the opportunity to trap your opponent.

219. Most tournament directors will allow deal-making. If you and your opponent are almost equal in chips, a deal might be a good idea—even if you believe you are the superior player—because the blinds will be so big that just a little bit of bad luck could land you in second place rather than first.

220. The way I like to make a deal if the chips are relatively evenly distributed is to divide about 80 to 90 percent of the money (first and second place combined) and then play for the remaining 10 or 20 percent, the title, and the bragging rights.

221. Deals also can be made with three, four, five, six or more players remaining. The deciding factor is that everyone must agree. Most of the time the director will stop the clock to allow for negotiations and will have a calculator if needed. They may even do the math for you.

222. Whenever any deal is made, notify the tournament director. This is just for insurance and he will be sure that everyone agrees and that everyone understands what he or she is agreeing on.

223. After winning, don't forget to tip. Many casinos and cardrooms will have a percentage added in for the dealers and other tournament employees. Ask what that amount is and then add what you are comfortable with. If it is a small buy-in tourney, a total of 7 to 10 percent is greatly appreciated. If you win a major tournament, 2 to 5 percent is good! See the suggestions on the tip amount in this chapter under "Tips for the Intermediate."

Now go forth and multiply those chips. Just remember, when you believe that you are good enough to turn pro, have a real job for backup!

2.

No-Limit Texas Hold'em

Not too many years ago, no-limit Texas hold'em was the big game played in the biggest poker tournament in the world, the World Series of Poker. That was about the extent of the game's popularity. Back then no-limit games were scarce except for big private games or at big poker tournaments in general, the World Series of Poker in particular. No-limit was a poker game most players feared. Only the best competitors with the most money played. Years ago, in 1978 to be precise, Doyle Brunson coined the phase, "No-limit hold'em is the Cadillac of poker games." In 1978 a Cadillac was the premier, top-of-the-line automobile. Brunson felt that way about the game of no-limit. Poker just doesn't get any better.

In the early seventies and eighties, the world champions would make appearances on national television shows but actual coverage of poker on TV didn't begin until years later and even at that, the game lacked excitement for viewers. The only folks with a real interest were the friends and loved ones of the participants.

In the late eighties, a few poker rooms in Las Vegas started hosting a few inexpensive weekly no-limit tournaments, just for fun. They were popular as were the usual games of limit hold'em, Omaha, and seven-card stud. Time has a way of changing things and things have certainly changed, especially in the world of poker. No-limit hold'em has captured the imagination of the world, far surpassing other games in popularity.

The explosion of interest in no-limit poker began in 2002 when the World Poker Tour aired its first season. The secret formula was the tiny "lipstick" cameras built into the poker table so the audience could see the players' holdings. Suddenly, it was fun and exciting to watch, and it became a spectator sport.

Today no-limit hold'em is one of the most popular games available, and it is the most mis-played game, all because TV allowed novices to get a fuller picture of the game being played without the all-important understanding of *why* professional players play the way they do. But read on, pay attention, study, and you will learn how to properly play this fascinating game that can literally change your life.

To reiterate, the basics of the games of limit hold'em and no-limit hold'em are the same. Two cards are dealt to each player beginning with the player to the right of the button (see table layout on page 2), followed by a round of betting, the flop, followed by a round of betting, the turn, followed by a round of betting, and last and possibly most importantly, the river, followed by a round of betting, and then the showdown to determine the winner. The similarities of the two games stop there.

Although the basics of no-limit hold'em are easy to learn, the game is the most complicated version of poker to play successfully. If you pay attention, follow the instructions in this book, and practice, practice, practice, you too can become a winning no-limit player.

No-Limit Hold'em Tips for the Beginner

224. My friend Chris Ferguson, the 2000 World Poker Champion, known to many as Jesus (because of his appearance), says this about playing poker, "You must love the game. Take your time and move up slowly. Playing poker can be a humbling experience; you learn real fast how to deal with failure. It's what you do with that failure that determines your future success."

225. Never, ever play with money you cannot afford to lose, especially while you are learning. Whatever you take to the poker table you should expect to double or more; however, just in case of a reversal in luck, before plopping money down to buy poker chips, ask yourself this question, "Can I afford to flush this money down the toilet?"

226. The basic and most obvious difference in limit and no-limit is how much you can bet. In limit games, you can bet according to the structure you are playing, for example $5-$10 or $30-$60. In no-limit you can bet any amount up to the amount you have in front of you.

227. I cannot stress enough how important it is to know your players. An unusually small raise from a good player should send up a warning flag—he wants a call—don't cooperate!

228. In limit hold'em you can make a mistake and survive. In no-limit, if you make one mistake you could be dead and gone (at least for that day or that tournament).

229. Don't be a calling station. There are players who seldom bet or raise, all they ever do if they are going to enter a pot is call. There is nothing wrong with calling occasionally, and sometimes it is the proper play, but if you always enter a pot with a call, you will never be a big winner. Calling is not aggressive, and aggression is important, especially in no-limit. Of course, you should always be *selectively* aggressive.

230. A very important factor in limit or no-limit is being able to read the board. When you are not involved in a hand, practice reading the board.

231. Example: The flop is K♣-4♦-3♣. What is the best possible hand? At this point it is a set of kings. The turn is a 5♥. Now the best possible hand is a seven high straight. The river is a 10♣. Now everything has changed and the nut hand is an ace-high flush!

232. Example: The flop is Q♦-J♣-4♥. What is the best possible hand? It is three queens. The turn brings a 2♦. The best hand remains three queens. The river changes everything because it is a 4♣. Now the best hand is quads. If there is someone with pocket queens, that person just made a full house for the second nut. If another player has pocket 4s, the full house is in big trouble.

233. What you should ask yourself in a game of no-limit is how much *should* I bet, rather than how much *can* I bet. The biggest mistake I see with new no-limit players is how they overbet or underbet the pot.

234. Do not just pick up a stack of chips and splash them in the pot. Think! "How much should I bet?" Your goal should be to maximize your wins but minimize your losses. This takes some thought.

235. Example: You have pocket aces under the gun. Now why on earth would you make a huge bet, run off all your customers, and pick up only the blinds?

236. You do not want to waste the profitability of your big hands because these hands normally are rare. Your goal should be to get one or two callers. Raise approximately three times the big blind. If someone raises you, reraise about the size of the pot.

237. If you pick up a big hand in late position and the pot has already been raised, just call if you believe you will be heads-up. Should you flop a monster like trip aces just check-call for more profit and then raise on the turn.

238. Example: You have pocket 6s in the cutoff seat. Three players have limped into the pot. Just call; do not raise. If the flop does not have a 6, you're finished with it. Even if the flop is all baby cards, do not call a bet. Minimize your losses.

239. Pairs from deuces to 10s should be played for as little investment as possible preflop. I wouldn't even play deuces through 6s from early position if there has been a lot of action at the table. If you are at a conservative table, go ahead and limp to see the flop, and then remember: no set, no bet.

240. Never play ace-little (ace with a card less than an 8) suited or unsuited in front position. If you bet and someone behind you raises, you're between a rock and a hard place. If they have an ace, their kicker is probably bigger than yours. If you check and he bets, you have the same dilemma.

241. It is okay to play ace-x (ace-little) suited in late position if the pot has not been raised. With everyone acting before it is your turn, you have more information. If an ace flops and it is checked to you, your ace is probably good, but if it is check-raised, minimize your losses.

242. However, if there is a big bet you can get away from the hand with a minimal investment. If the flop brings two of your suit, you can decide whether or not to take the fourth card by the action in front of you. If checked, good, you get a free card. If bet, it will depend on the amount of the bet for you to make your decision whether to call or fold.

243. Calling a bet with a drawing hand, a flush draw, or a straight draw also depends on pot odds. (We will get into pot odds in the advanced study of this game.)

244. You can win pots much more often before the flop in no-limit hold'em than in limit hold'em. In limit, if a player in middle position has a big hand and raises and you have a big hand and reraise, he will call to see the flop. In no-limit you can raise enough to make him fold and possibly not see the flop that would have turned into a winner for him.

245. Remember, if you bet, raise, or reraise and do not get a caller, you cannot lose the pot. That is a fine scenario if you have medium to weak holdings or if you're on a draw. There will be times that you do want a caller, so bet or check accordingly.

246. Example: You are on the button with pocket queens. The blinds are $2-$4 and a player from middle position puts in an $8 raise. In limit you could reraise only to $12 and in all likelihood you would get a call; but in no-limit you can make it $35 to go. Unless your opponent has aces or kings or is a yahoo, he is going to fold and you will pick up the blinds plus his $8. This is called protecting your hand.

247. You will have to fold many hands from early position in no-limit as a general rule, but you can raise with these very hands from late position when no one has opened the pot. Example: K-10, Q-J, A-X, K-J, J-10.

248. Drawing to make a hand in no-limit is very different from drawing to the same hands in limit. In limit you would rarely fold a four straight or a four flush, especially if your draw is to the nuts. But in no-limit drawing could cost you all of your chips.

249. The time to consider such draws in no-limit is in multiway pots where you can draw relatively inexpensively—but only if you are drawing to the nuts. It's even sweeter when you are drawing to the nuts and also have a pair.

250. Example: You are in late position with a J-10. The flop comes K-Q-4, rainbow (different suits.) You are drawing to an ace for the nut straight or to a 9. The turn brings a 10 so now you have a pair and a good draw. The odds have turned more and more in your favor.

251. In no-limit do not commit half your chips to the pot unless you are willing to go all the way and commit all of your chips. In other words, don't overbet your hand.

252. Example: You have $80 in front of you. You are in middle position with an A-Q; you raise the opening bet to $10. If someone raises to $45, do not call unless you are willing to invest your full $80. If you are willing, then reraise all in. I don't recommend this with an A-Q.

253. Try to never go all in on a call. You want to be the one putting on the pressure. If you go all in, it should be your bet, raise, or a reraise.

254. This is a perfect example of how important it is to know your players. If the player who raised you is a rock, you know you must fold. If he is a bully you might decide to reraise.

255. When considering whether or not to enter the pot from early to middle position, ask yourself a question, "If this pot is raised, can I call the raise?" If the answer is no, then do not enter the pot in the first place.

256. You will notice that many players will raise every time they have the button. They are not good players. They just think that having the button is an automatic raise rule. It's not. Think before making a raise.

257. Above all else, no-limit is a game of guts. Some men believe this means women can't play well. Many good female players will stomp on these men. It doesn't take a beer belly or testosterone to have guts!

258. A hint for the men: beware of the female player. There are a zillion differences between men and women in life. There is just one difference between men and women at the poker table—women have breasts. But as is always true in poker, there is an exception to every rule. Some men also have breasts to go along with their beer bellies.

259. Women are at the poker table for the same reason men are there, to win the money while having a good time. Men who think women are weak at the poker table are giving those women a huge advantage.

260. Always remember that it does not take brawn to have brains. The poker table is the only completely level playing field.

261. Beware of early position limpers. They could have a hand too big to bet and be setting a trap that you don't want to step into.

262. Playing middle suited (8-7, 10-9, J-10) from up front is a big no-no. Play them from late position only if there has been no raise, and personally I wouldn't play them unless I was well ahead of the game. If you do play them, continue after the flop only if you flopped perfect.

263. If you never lay down a winning hand, you're playing too loose. If you never lay down the winner you're playing way too many hands and you'll be losing a lot too. The idea is to win the ones you play. Be selective.

264. Don't be afraid to try a bluff or a semibluff now and then. How else will you know what you can get away with? Just like a naughty child, keep it up until you get caught and punished and then back off.

265. On your bluffing excursions, don't be reckless. Pick and choose your moments. Example: You're in the cutoff seat and have a fold tell on the button or you have an ace-rag in the big blind and the button always raises, pop him back!

266. Sometimes the bluff will be a mistake, but do not fret; let it go and move on. The best player in the world will make a mistake now and then. Your goal is to play as mistake-free as possible. He who makes the least mistakes will win the most money.

267. Most people do not realize the value of picking up the blinds with a raise from late position. As previously mentioned, you should not raise every time you are on the button, but you also should take advantage of good position as often as possible. Done often enough, it adds up for a minimal risk.

268. If you are playing with low funds after a few losses, you need to tighten up. If you have a nice stack of chips in front of you after a few wins, you can loosen up—maybe even throw in an occasional bluff or semibluff from late position when the time is right.

269. This holds true for ring games or tournament play. In tournament competition, the higher the limit, the more chips you can accumulate with blind stealing.

270. Speaking of tournament play, the basics of the four stages in a poker tournament discussed in limit hold'em hold true in no-limit as well. The stages include the beginning, the middle, and the late stages, and end with final table success. I'll advise you on the differences in strategies in limit and no-limit tournaments.

271. My friend Dr. Max Stern holds several world titles. I have seen Max raise all in after the flop with the nut flush draw in a no-limit tournament. This is a semibluff. He picked up the pot then and there. While he is the type of player to make such a move at any stage of the tournament, I won't risk all my chips on a draw early in competition.

272. It is just as important, if not more so, to wait and observe in the early stages of a no-limit tournament as it is in limit. If you get involved in any hand early in limit, you can survive, but if you do the same in no-limit you have the possibility of going broke or being severely wounded. In tournament play, it's best to start the race in a low, slow gear.

273. True story: My friend Bill Fain from Virginia City, Nevada, was coming to Las Vegas some years back to play in the $10,000 main event of the World Series of Poker. This is an exciting time for any poker player and even more so when it is a maiden voyage. Bill was running just a tad late. He rushed in, hurried up to his seat, and picked up his two cards before he sat down. He was looking at two red aces. The pot had been raised in front of him and reraised all in. To call it would take his entire stack of $10,000.

274. Not many people would lay *that* hand down preflop in any situation, but Bill said later, "I know aces can be beaten. I couldn't stand the thought of getting them cracked and having to leave before I even took my coat off and sat down. I hadn't even had time to look around and get the juices flowing with the excitement of this wonderful tournament. I decided I had plenty of time and I preferred to tell the story of laying down those two aces than taking the chance of having to tell a horrible beat on the first hand I ever got to play in my first opportunity to play the big one."

275. In almost any poker tournament you play, big buy-in or small, you will most likely run into what I call the "young guns." These are the young aggressive players who constantly mimic the type of poker player we see on TV.

276. These novices often will wear sunglasses and a hat trying to be cool and look tough. They move full speed ahead at all times, but just wait; they eventually will shoot themselves in the foot and limp away from the table, leaving their chips in someone else's stack.

277. Most of the time, people do not realize that the poker competition they are watching on TV is the end of a tournament. Not only are they watching the end, but also the final table that has been edited from about three or four hours of play into approximately fifty-two minutes. The producers are showing only the exciting hands. It is a mirage and not the way tournament poker is actually played.

278. There also are the young guns who know how to slow down. They are often successful with their overly aggressive style because they are smart enough to know when to change gears. They know when they are pushing the limit and they know when to back off. These guys are dangerous players. Proceed with caution.

279. I do not advocate bowing down to a bully. Rather, wait until the time is right, when you are looking at a pair or a good draw, and after he makes his usual raise, move all in. Now the decision rests on him. You must be willing to go broke in order to accumulate chips (and put a bully in his place). This is called big-bet poker.

280. Once you make the decision, any all-in bet is the easiest in no-limit. You have no more decisions to make on the hand and the pressure is on your opponent. Try not to call all in, though. Whenever possible, make the all-in play with a raise or a reraise.

281. Survival is the key to winning no-limit tournaments and that requires knowing when to hold'em and when to fold'em. Sometimes you will have to make difficult laydowns in order to survive. You cannot win the tournament if you're not in the tournament.

282. Around the fifth or sixth level in no-limit tournaments, you will be anteing in addition to putting in your blinds. This is true of *real* tournaments, not necessarily small buy-in weekly events or Internet competition. Your goal should be to survive until that level and then start playing.

283. Example: When the level reaches $100-$200 blinds, the next level should be $100-$200 with a $25 ante. The next level will go to $150-$300 with a $50 ante and then $200-$400 with a $75 ante and on up.

284. Now is the time to start some bluffing and semibluffing because based on the blinds and antes, every hand is an established pot (something worth winning). Hold your breath and jump in.

285. It is scary to push all your chips into the pot from late position with only a marginal hand, but it is often necessary in order to survive while waiting on "real" hands. Many pros say that after so many years, it isn't so scary. I've been playing major tournaments since 1991, and I'm still waiting.

286. If you can pick up one hand a round, you can stay ahead of the game. If that doesn't happen, don't panic; you might pick up two the next round and then, boom, you might pick up a monster. Play it just right to maximize your profit and suddenly you can breathe easy for a while.

287. In the middle stages of a tournament, you should be building and protecting your chip stack.

288. If something goes wrong on a hand and you lose a chunk of your hard-earned chips, do not panic. One thing I love about no-limit is that you can be the shortest stack at the table and within three hands become the chip leader.

289. Many times I have seen players get in a comfort zone with the amount of chips they have been accumulating throughout the tourney. Then they take a bad beat from a yahoo and go on tilt. They blow the rest of their chips off in disgust and go home in a huff. Do not make this mistake. As long as you have a chip, you have a chance.

290. One of the toughest hands for me to play in a no-limit tourney is A-K. Most players treat it as if it is a huge pair, but the fact is that preflop, a baby pair is bigger.

291. Play big slick very gingerly early in the tournament, a bit more aggressively in the middle rounds, and much more aggressively later in the tournament, especially in shorthanded play.

292. I would alternate raising and calling with A-K from early or middle position in the middle rounds of a tourney. If you just pick up the blinds, good. If you hit a flop, wonderful, but if you raise and get a caller and the flop comes with rags or paints that miss you, do not bet unless your opponent is ultra-conservative. If you do bet, put in a "test" bet, especially if he has checked to you.

293. If you decide to play A-K in short-handed play, move all in. That way you will get to see all five cards—or you'll pick up the pot preflop.

294. As noted in the limit hold'em section, don't forget to watch the clock as it gets later in the tournament. In the early stages you've got plenty of time. In the later stages that clock becomes of vital importance, especially if you are short-stacked.

295. My Mama used to say that the secret to a good sixty-five-year marriage was flexibility. I say that the secret to winning poker tournaments is also flexibility.

296. No one who plays the same for the entirety of a tournament will be a winner. You must change your style to keep others confused and to adjust to the style of your opponents.

297. As you near the money and then the final table in a no-limit tournament, your goal is either to win it outright or to move up in the ranks. My philosophy is to move up in the rankings one step at a time.

298. With every hand you consider playing, stop and ask yourself: will I win this hand or is this a bonehead play that will knock me out of the competition?

299. If you have enough chips for survival then play just premium hands or take advantage of late position bluffing in order to keep moving up. If you are short-stacked, pick your best opportunity and go for it—all in.

300. You will find that as you get near the money, players will tighten up in order to make the money; and once you make the money, almost everyone will start playing again. Watch them. Be very observant of how everyone is playing.

301. If you know a player is interested only in moving up one notch at a time, you can attack his blinds. If you know a player is interested only in making first place, he will be playing looser so don't be afraid to move in on him with A-Q or any pair.

302. Don't let a loose player bully you off a hand. Take a stand. If you lose the hand you will still win some money, and if you win you will have more ammunition to go for the bigger money.

303. Once you get to the final table you should seldom limp into a pot. As a matter of fact, if a good player does limp into a pot, beware! He probably has big holdings.

304. If there are short stacks at your final table, try to wait until they are gone, causing you to move up in the money. If you have chips, you can attack the short stacks, and if you are the short stack, jump in, all in with any ace or any pair. Hopefully that will get you back in the game.

305. If you are low chipped, any paint is playable, provided no one has made a big move at the pot before the action gets to you. The exception is if the bully has a huge stack and is raising virtually every pot.

306. I personally believe making deals at the final table of a poker tournament is a good idea. Deals are made in a number of ways. If everyone is about even in chips, chop up the money equally. If one player has a tremendous chip lead, offer him more and the rest of you cut up the remaining amount. If everyone is uneven in chips but all want to deal, you can go by chip count.

307. The tournament director can tell you the value of each chip and you can calculate accordingly. Be sure you get more than you would if you played it out.

308. Example: Let's say there are six players remaining and you have the short stack when the deal is proposed. The other players elect to go by chip count but when the figuring is finished you will win $700, but sixth place would pay $720. That makes it a foolish deal for you, so veto it. If they want to deal with you they need to offer you at least 10 percent more than what you normally would get.

309. When you get to heads up and a deal has not yet been made, I suggest some wheeling and dealing if you are so inclined. The levels can get so high that continuing to play becomes more like a crapshoot than a poker tournament.

310. So lock up the best deal you can and then continue to play your heart out. Deal or no deal, you want to win first place.

311. You should note that the World Poker Tour does not allow deals and the World Series bracelet cannot be included in a deal.

312. There is no greater thrill for a poker player than winning a major tournament. I realize that the average player cannot shell out $5,000 or $10,000 to even participate in a major event, but there are a number of inexpensive ways to get that buy-in. We'll get into that shortly, so read on, my friends.

313. Knowing your opponents and how they play is critical in no-limit since it is as much a game of playing the people as playing the cards. Watch what is going on at your table and size up your opponents. Remember: you cannot bluff the unbluffable, so choose your moments wisely.

314. There is one ingredient for becoming a good player that cannot be taught. That is a feeling or an intuition as to whether someone is bluffing you or when it is time for you to bluff. The great players just know.

315. The only way to know is to listen to your inner voice, pay attention to your gut feelings and act upon them. If you are right most of the time, you have that edge, if you are not, just practice playing good poker.

316. Bluffing is of greater importance in no-limit than in limit because you can't bet enough in limit to make your opponent stop, think, and possibly fold. In limit there are many brainless calls when the pot is raised. In no-limit you can bet enough to get their attention.

317. 1982 World Champion Jack Strauss said, "Consider limit hold'em a science; you're shooting at a target. Consider no-limit hold'em an art; the target comes alive and shoots back at you!"

318. As for the rocks, they don't have the heart to play true no-limit. They wait for the nut hands and then, when they raise, they don't get any action because they are rocks.

319. A good no-limit poker player is not afraid to play a pot. As a matter of fact, there are more playable hands in no-limit than in limit hold'em because of the pot odds. The pots get so big in no-limit that often a jack-10 or even small-suited connectors are worth calling a reasonable raise if you are in late position.

320. In a ring game of no-limit with a buy-in of $200, if you get involved in a big hand and go broke, rebuy to stay in the game for another $200 only if the game is good. If there is enough action that you can easily make $400 (your original investment) or more, the rebuy is worth it.

321. If it is a very tight, slow game, try again another day. Another alternative is to change tables. Look for greener pastures.

322. Do not check a big hand from early position, unless you are sure an aggressive player behind you will bet. Checking to some players is like waving a red flag at a bull; they will bet! If that happens, then check-raise those players.

323. At times you may bet not because you think you have the best hand but because you want to gain information. And sometimes that bet will win the pot for you then and there.

324. Example: You are in the big blind with a Q♥-5♣. The pot is unraised so you get to see a free flop. There are two players and yourself. The flop comes 6♠-4♣-3♥. The flop missed you completely, but did it hit anybody else? A bet will gain that information—and you have an open-ended straight in case someone just calls you. This is a semibluff. You are bluffing but you have outs.

325. Another example: You are in middle position with K♣-J♦. The flop comes A♦-J♥-5♠. There are three players in the pot. The first one checks to you. You bet to see if either of them has an ace.

326. Playing ace-X suited from early to middle position depends on the texture of your table. If players are allowing limping, try to see a cheap flop (unraised). If it's a really tight table, put in a raise to steal the blinds. However, if it's a ramming, jamming game with a lot of preflop raising, wait for a better hand and/or better position.

327. Calling a raise or reraising is entirely different than opening the pot with a raise. At a conservative table you likely would raise with A-J from middle position, maybe even from early position, but you wouldn't (absolutely shouldn't) reraise or call a raise.

328. Whether in tournaments or ring games, never soft-play anybody. If you are at a table with your lifelong friend who is the godmother of your children, you gotta do it—bust her!

329. The only exception to this rule is in a penny ante home game. If your great grandmother is in the game, it's okay. You can soft-play her—a little.

330. It's useful to develop a conservative image, but you should vary your play—if you think you can bluff grandma and get her to fold, do it!

331. There is no set mold that makes a winning no-limit player. Some winning players have an aggressive style; some have a more conservative style.

332. There is a set mold for losing players. These are the maniacs, the rocks, and the calling stations.

333. The aggressive winning player knows when to put on the brakes. The conservative winning players know when to speed things up. It's called changing gears and is much more prevalent (and necessary) in tournament competition.

334. The good player knows when to change gears, based on information he has gathered on how his opponents are playing, their styles, tells, positions, and his own position. In a tournament it also depends on what stage you are in and the size of your opponent's chip stacks.

335. Watch out for the rocks although they are pretty easy to play. You simply don't go up against them unless you have a powerhouse.

336. On the flip side of that coin, you should also watch out for the maniacs. They are much more difficult to play because it is so difficult to "put them on" a hand, that is, determine what cards they may be playing.

337. Maniacs seem to be playing for fun and action, not necessarily to win. Depending on the limits they are playing, it can seem as if they have a money tree somewhere or an inheritance (a big one!).

338. I preach solid play; however, you should mix it up a bit. Never become predictable. Throw some zigs and zags into your play. Keep them confused. Just when they believe they have you pegged as a conservative player who never gets out of line, get out of line. Keep them off guard.

339. I have heard it said that the only difference between a solid player and a maniac is the frequency of their risky business. You have to take that risk now and then.

340. There have been a lot of young guns over the last few years who have been very successful playing like an out-of-control Mack truck—full speed ahead with full force. Will this style keep them in the winner's circle for years to come? I don't know. Ask me in twenty years. I'm doubtful.

341. Time will tell about the life expectancy of the Mack trucks. I have seen "my" style—solid play with an occasionally bold move—endure through the decades.

342. The bluff is a very important part of the no-limit game, but the less you bluff, the more effective your bluffs will be (against good players). Timing is everything.

343. I harp about playing against good players so much because most often a strategy that will work against an experienced player will go unnoticed against a yahoo. Sophisticated plays need to be made against sophisticated players.

344. Doyle Brunson says, "When bluffing, always have an out. I prefer to have many outs."

345. Example: You call a small raise in a four-way pot in late position with a 10♦-9♣. The flop comes 8♠-7♦-3♦. Everyone checks to you. Now is the time to bluff. Bet about the size of the pot. You have many outs. You could catch a 6 or a jack for a straight or a 9 or a 10 to pair for top pair, but the idea is to take the pot then and there. Consider your outs your insurance—just in case someone calls your bluff.

346. Never show a bluff. Players who run a successful bluff and then show their nothing cards consider it "advertising" so they can then set up a player with a good hand. I do not agree with this strategy.

347. I not only advocate never showing a bluff, I believe in never showing a hand unless you have to. Why? Because you're giving away too much information.

348. Many players take great pride in showing their bluffs or showing their hands, win or lose. Pay attention when this happens. The more information you can get on how your opponent plays, the better. The less you give up about how you play, the better.

349. Limping in on the small blind is fine if your opponent will allow it. As a matter of fact, I limp as often as possible in the blind or from late position for two reasons: 1) to see as many flops as possible and 2) so I can limp when I pick up a monster hand and set a trap.

350. Sometimes when attempting to set a trap, you end up trapping yourself. Think it through and be careful. Be cautious when slow-playing a big hand if there is a good draw on the board.

351. Example: In a full ring game, if you pick up two red aces in late position, you want to bet or raise just the right amount to end up playing against no more than two opponents or, preferably, to be heads up (playing against only one opponent).

352. Let's say the flop comes A♣-9♦-3♣. You want to trap with your huge set of aces. However, be careful about those clubs, especially if you are against two other players. Put in a nice-size bet or raise about the size of the pot if you are up against one player or make it a slightly bigger bet if you're against two or more players. If anybody is going for clubs, make them pay for it.

353. Same hand only this time you're heads-up in a tournament. Slow-play until the river. If you can't get your opponent to bet then make a medium-size bet on the river (half the size of the pot). Ideally, you will check the flop, he will bet the turn, and you can raise a healthy sum.

354. Any time you're shorthanded or heads up in a tournament, slow-play any big pair. Yes, you're gambling, but you need to try to maximize those opportunities.

355. Comparing ring game play to tournament play is like comparing golf to football. Truly, there is that much difference and if you understand the whys and wherefores, and have the stamina, patience, guts, and heart to compete properly in tournament competition, you will either love it or hate it.

356. I love poker tournaments because of the tremendous overlay opportunities. If I take $200 into a ring game (live game versus tournament) of no-limit Texas hold'em, play for three hours, and double or triple my money, I had a good session. However, for the same $200 investment, I can have the opportunity to win much, much more in a poker tournament and if all goes well, I will get to play for huge limits that I would never be able to afford in a ring game.

357. The likelihood of winning tens of thousands of dollars by putting your poker prowess to the task in a poker tournament is a much longer shot than the likelihood of a good player winning hundreds or even a thousand or two in a ring game. However, somebody is going to win that tournament! Why not you? If you don't buy the lottery ticket, you do not have a chance of that miracle happening; winning a poker tournament is a much more likely bet, especially for a skillful player.

358. Keep in mind, you do not have to win first place to win a lot of money. Most tournaments are now paying one spot for every ten players, which means that in a tournament with three hundred fifty participants, thirty-five players will have a payday. In a tournament with one hundred twenty players, twelve will be paid and so forth. In most small buy-in weekly tournaments ($100 or less) in Las Vegas, if the field tops one hundred, they will pay two tables—eighteen or twenty players.

359. Major tournaments need to be played in four stages, the early stages (rounds 1, 2, and 3), the middle stages (rounds 5, 6, and 7), the late stages (rounds 7, 8, 9, and up), and the final table. With the exception of the early stages, you will need to do a lot of changing gears.

360. Play the early stages of a no-limit tournament just as you would a ring game. Your early play should be solid, conservative, and selectively aggressive. There is no need to take risks or gamble early in any tournament.

361. In the middle stages, rev it up a notch while dodging any runaway trains (maniacs). Pick up the blinds when you can and proceed cautiously.

362. In fast-paced tournaments (small buy-ins with shorter rounds), it's basically a game of raise or fold by the time you hit the middle rounds. In tournaments with a slower structure, you have time to play and plenty of time to maneuver.

363. In the late stages you should be speeding up, slowing down, speeding up, and slowing down. What you do when depends on whom you are against and what they will let you get away with.

364. Often when they are just one or two places away from the money, many players will slow way down in an effort just to make the money. This is a good time to steal a lot of pots.

365. It can be very disheartening to play your best for ten hours (there are potty breaks and a break for meals, depending on the length of the event) only to end up on the dreaded bubble. It is terribly disappointing and can bring a tear to a grown man's eye.

366. However, when you do taste that thrill of victory, the high can last for days. If it is a major tournament, you'll find yourself floating around on that victory cloud for weeks.

367. Keep in mind: you don't have to be crowned the champion to go home with a nice chunk of change. The big money is usually in the top three spots, but any score should be considered a feather in your cap.

368. Late in a tournament, always know the chip stacks of all your opponents. At the very least know how many players have a smaller stack than yours.

369. You can have a sweater (one who is watching and rooting for you) be your look out and give you hand signals—holding up the number of fingers of how many players remain who have shorter stacks than you, for example. This is not cheating. It is getting as much information as possible to help in your decision-making. It is smart play.

370. This information will help you decide how you want to play at any given time. If you are one away from a prize increase and four players have shorter stacks than you, you want to wait. If you are the shortest stack, you have to make a move.

371. If you are interested in playing big buy-in tournaments or the WSOP or the World Poker Tour but your pocketbook says no (remember the rule: play only with money you can afford to flush), there are alternatives.

372. If you live in an area that has casinos, the poker rooms probably run satellites for the larger tournaments. A satellite is a tournament with a smaller buy-in that parlays the win into the buy-in for the major event.

373. I believe satellites are wonderful. So many of us cannot afford the big buy-in events, but we can get there through these parlay opportunities.

374. Example: A supersatellite is a multi-table satellite that will award the number of seats that the prize pool allows. Let's say the buy-in is $230 ($200 goes to the prize pool and $30 goes to the house to pay expenses). They allow rebuys that cost $200 each for the first hour of play. You are playing for a $10,000 seat to the WSOP. After the first hour, the loot is counted and the prizes are announced.

375. If there are two hundred twenty players, then the basic prize pool is $44,000. If there are 453 rebuys, another $90,600 is added to the prize pool for a total of $134,600. They would award thirteen seats, a $10,000 value each, and divide the remaining $4,600 as prize money for fourteenth, fifteenth, sixteenth, and on down the line depending on their formula for prize fund distribution. They might divide the overage among the winners for travel expenses if the supersatellite is held somewhere besides Las Vegas.

376. Supersatellites are high-speed tournaments. Sit down, fasten your seat belt, and pray. I prefer one-table satellites where the field is much smaller.

377. A one-table satellite is another parlay opportunity. If you were playing for a $1,000 seat, you would pay approximately $120 each and have to beat only nine players.

378. Deals are commonplace in one-table satellites. If it gets down to two players and one has the majority of the chips, he may offer his opponent a few hundred dollars to go away. If they are relatively close in chip position, one may pay the other $500 for the win. That way they both win half their buy-in.

379. When it's down to only two players, you may agree on a deal that one of you will play the tournament but give up a percentage of his action to his opponent. If this is the case and you know that your opponent is a stronger player than you, make the deal!

380. One-table satellites usually consist of fifteen-minute rounds. Conservative play is okay, but only for the first round or round and a half.

381. In the first few rounds players will be eliminated. After that you will have to play faster than normal and learn how to stay out of the way in some pots.

382. One-table satellites involve playing your players, a lot of zigging and zagging, and more luck than in a normal tournament. After the fourth round you will probably be moving all in if you enter a pot.

383. Don't be totally reckless but remember, as the field gets shorter, your starting hand requirements are greatly reduced. By the time you are heads up, you want to raise with any ace, any paint, and any pair. Unless you pick up aces or kings, then slow-play before the flop.

384. Whatever two cards you are holding, if you flop favorably, slow-play and try to get your opponent to move in—you call—you win! (Hopefully.)

385. If your opponent will allow it, call the big blind with almost any two cards. Anything can flop. I can't tell you how many one-table satellites I have won by just calling the big blind with any two cards and catching a good flop. Trap City!

386. If you don't live near a casino that offers satellites, don't fret. In chapter 10, I'll give you detailed instructions so that you can have your own, right at home.

387. Let's begin our advanced study of my favorite game with Susie's Five P Theory. If you follow the Five P Theory to the letter, you will be a winning player.

388. 1. Patience: So easy to understand but so difficult to execute. Remember, you cannot win a poker tournament in the first few rounds, but you sure can lose it! Wait for the proper starting hands.

389. 2. Position: Not so easy for beginners to understand but such a strong defensive tool once you get it. Knowing what your opponents are going to do before the betting gets to you is very valuable information. A hand you may toss in early position you could just as easily raise with in late position.

390. 3. Psychology: The psychological aspect of poker, playing the players and your position rather than your cards, is a bit more advanced. It's the same with picking up tells and using them as a defensive tool.

391. 4. Perseverance: Never give up! The beats are part of the game. Think forward, not in reverse. You must have some luck to go with your skill, but I guarantee you need more skill to go with your luck to be a winning player. (Of course, "never give up" doesn't mean you don't know when to fold or call it a night. Play smart.)

392. 5. Practice: Play, play, and play if you want to be a student of the game. Make notes and study them. The knowledge you develop from situational play is ammunition for the future.

393. Advanced poker playing is psychological warfare, especially in no-limit, because you can make such big bets that it really puts the pressure on. Even if you don't have the biggest hand, your bet could dictate that you do. You also can make bets big enough to get an opponent off a straight or a flush draw. You cannot do that in limit hold'em.

394. No-limit is a game of trapping and bluffing. Your goal is to set good traps but avoid stepping into a trap. You should bluff when the time is right, but avoid being bluffed.

395. You should seldom bluff in a ring game. Seldom does not mean never. If you are playing with good players, your play will be respected and when you do decide to make a move, your bluffs will have power.

396. Money management must be practiced both on and off the poker table. I know poker players who have won millions of dollars playing poker but have blown it all in the sports book or at the craps table.

397. Skill, discipline, money management, and some luck will help get you to the top. It also takes heart. That one is a bit hard to explain. Think of those children's rubber dolls that won't knock down. You hit them, they go down, but come right back up. (You can't let the bad beats get you down.)

398. A talented ring game player does not always make for a great tournament player and vice versa. In ring games you play basically in the same solid gear, changing only occasionally when opportunity knocks. If you use this strategy in a tournament, you will be gobbled up in the later rounds. You must learn the talent of bobbing and weaving (changing gears) and when to do what in order to be successful in poker tournaments.

399. Whether playing an intuitive or an analytical game, the ins, outs, odds, and probabilities are all very important. Just as important, if not more so, is refining your ability to read your opponents. The way to do this is to watch and play, play and watch.

400. Unlike figuring pot odds, there is no formula for figuring "people odds." Is the player betting big because he has a big hand, or is he betting big because he doesn't want a caller? Watch to see if you can pick up the tiniest hint that will answer that question and you will win most of the confrontations against that player. More on this subject in chapter 9, "Tells."

401. When you have an opportunity to play in a major tournament, you need to prepare yourself in more than the knowledge of how to play tournament poker. The best of cars will not run if they are not maintained or if they run out of gas. Likewise, the best of poker players cannot perform at their best if they are not prepared.

402. If you travel to participate in a big poker tournament, arrive a few days early to allow your body to adjust to the time zone.

403. Do not play too many hours of poker in the days prior to a big competition.

404. Do not drink alcohol for a few days before the event or during play!

405. Be well rested. Go into a tournament after a light, healthy breakfast. Bring nuts and protein bars with you. Eat a light, healthy meal for dinner.

406. During competition, take the time to think about a major decision (like putting all your chips into the pot). Ask yourself if you are making a mistake or if it would be a mistake to fold. Ask yourself how much you should bet or raise and why.

407. Make no knee-jerk plays. Wait until the time is right and make the correct decisions.

408. In a major tournament, you will get away with what other players will allow, so get to know how they play. If you have some superaggressive players at your table, you will be forced to "be good," play in a low gear, and not get out of line. If you pick up a big hand against one or both of them, your goal will be to maximize your win.

409. Do not overplay your hand. Let them believe that if they keep betting or raising you will go away. When the time is right, reraise them—throw it into high gear.

410. Example: You are holding A♥-K♠. An aggressive player has raised and another has called. Just call. The flop is A♦-K♣-2♣. The first player bets, the second folds, you should just call. The turn is a 7♥. The lead player makes a big bet. Now is the time to make your move; it is very unlikely he has you beat. You know this by the way he has been playing. He probably is holding ace-rag. Now, go for the jugular. Hopefully he has an ace-deuce and thinks he is gold. You get all the money. This is a perfect example of not overplaying your hand in order to maximize your profit.

411. Mix up your play, keep your opponents off-guard; don't be predictable. Occasionally limp in and sometimes fold when it is raised behind you. This gives you trap-setting potential.

412. Never over-commit yourself to the pot with a marginal hand, a bluff, or a semibluff. If you bet more than half your stack, you are pot committed. If you plan to make a raise on a marginal hand, a bluff, or a semibluff, you are doing so because you think your opponent(s) will fold. If you bet less than 50 percent of your stack, you can get away from your hand if someone, particularly a solid player, plays back at you. If you have 60 or 70 percent of your chips in the pot, you are pot committed. If you're going to put that much into the pot, go ahead and move all in.

413. The exception to this rule is if you have a big hand and know you'll put all your chips in the pot on any reraise. Then it is okay to put yourself in a pot-committed situation, especially if you're looking for a caller.

414. There is nothing sweeter than being at the final table with a medium stack, picking up a monster, and trapping the big stack that has a good hand. Voila! You magically become the big stack, and he becomes a medium stack.

415. My friend, poker guru Rick Gianti, explains a poker tournament thusly: "Consider the tournament big game hunting and your chips are your ammunition. If you waste your ammunition messing around and shooting at trees and beer bottles, then when the big game comes along you may not have enough ammunition to bag your trophy."

416. In tournament play you cannot buy more chips (unless it's a rebuy tourney). You can get more chips only by winning them. With this in mind, treat your chips like precious and irreplaceable gems. As the tournament progresses, they become even more valuable.

417. In any stage of a tourney a rush is wonderful, but you can never depend on a rush. You need to recognize when another player is on a rush and avoid getting involved in pots with such a player. Also learn to recognize when his rush is over.

418. If you are lucky enough to get on a rush, milk it for all it's worth. When it is over, change gears accordingly. Never overplay a rush. Hold on to those precious gems (chips).

419. Think! Unless it is an automatic fold, each decision is crucial, particularly in tournament competition because you cannot buy more chips if you go broke. In no-limit you can go broke on any hand at any time, so think!

420. No matter how hard you try to make the correct decisions every time, there will be times that you will make the right decision but the result will not be in your favor. Some right moves are made at the wrong time, and some wrong moves are made at the right time.

421. My poker professor Tom McEvoy says, "Unlike limit poker, in which you have to win a series of pots and show down lots of hands, in no-limit hold'em you don't have to win lots of pots; you just have to win most of the ones you play. And you don't have to play very many hands."

422. More McEvoy wisdom: "Don't let fear freeze your play. People who don't gamble enough usually are afraid of getting knocked out of a tournament, but there is another way to look at things. Whether you get knocked out one place out of the money or first makes no difference. The result is the same."

423. "Throughout the entire tournament, you must be playing to win and trying to accumulate chips so that you can make the money. Don't worry about getting knocked out. Play to win or don't play at all."

424. "Using position, chip power, and good timing is often more important than getting good cards in no-limit. In other words, you can win pots with no cards." (Figuratively speaking!)

425. It is worth repeating that it may be a tough decision to make but once you make it, the easiest move in no-limit is when you move all in. You have no more decisions to make. You will win the pot then and there or you will get to see all five-community cards. You have put the decision on your opponent.

426. Your decision to move all in will depend on several factors: you think you have the winning hand and you do not want your opponent to draw to a hand that can beat you, you're short-stacked and have to make a move, or your odds of making a winning hand are good enough to justify this risk.

427. To determine the odds of making your hand, you must first know your outs. Outs are the number of cards that you believe will make your hand the winning hand.

428. You need to have a read on what your opponent is holding in order to determine if the hand you are trying to make will be the winning hand. If you can make your hand and your opponent still beats you, it is called drawing dead.

429. Each time you play a hand you must consider the strength of your hand in relation to the cards on the board and what hand you believe your opponent is holding. If you believe you must improve your hand to win (you put him on a big pair and you have an open-ended straight or a flush draw), you then must figure the percentage for improving your hand based on the number of outs you have.

430. To be precise in calculating your odds of making a hand, you have to be a quick mathematician or have a calculator at the poker table. When you see the major league players thinking and thinking about a decision on television, they often are figuring their odds of making a hand.

431. My friend, poker player and columnist Jan Fisher, offered her readers a simple formula, which, though not exact, is very close. With two cards to come after the flop you multiply your number of outs by four. With one card to come after the turn, you multiply your number of outs by two.

432. Example: If you have a four-card flush after the flop, you have nine outs. With two cards to come, multiply the nine by four and you get a 36 percent chance of making the flush. With one card to come, you multiply nine by two and you have an 18 percent chance.

433. This formula is not exact but it is easy to do in your mind. The idea is to try to make a mathematical estimation of the likelihood of catching the card that will give you the winning hand and determine whether it is worth the risk.

434. Another thing to consider: If your opponent has put himself all in with his bet on the flop and no one else has entered the pot, you know exactly how much it is going to cost you to see the flop, the turn, and the river. This greatly improves your odds.

435. Deal making at the final table is probably more important in no-limit tournaments than in any other simply because you can go broke on any given hand.

436. Example: You have arrived at the final table and you are in average chip position but there are two very short stacks at the table. Wait until they either go out or one or both of them begins to rebuild their chips, then suggest a deal.

437. If one player says, "I'm not interested," then you cannot take negotiations any further. However, if that player is then eliminated, you can once again ask about a deal. Some players are against a deal under any circumstances while others are always willing.

438. Example: You are at the final table and there are six of you remaining. One player has a very large stack; the other five are close to each other in their chip count. The remaining prize pool is $90,000. You could propose that the big stack receive $25,000 and each of you remaining receive $15,000 each. That would leave $5,000 to play for.

439. Remember with a short field (five or six players) at the final table you have fewer combinations of cards competing against you and fewer challengers. For instance, a small pair at the final table with a short field is comparable to a big pair early in the tournament. Any ace late in the tourney is comparable to big slick early on.

440. The shorter the field, the lower your starting-hand requirements should be. It is high-gear time. Be aggressive unless you think you are beat, and then save as many chips as you can.

441. When you make the final table of a major event you most likely will be on TV. Lights, microphones, cameras, and a live audience will surround you. It won't be easy, but you must get into a poker-playing zone, blocking out all the excitement that is surrounding you.

442. After you win, it also isn't easy to re-enter the real world and let the excitement flow. Take a deep breath, and think about what you have accomplished. Then let her rip—Yahooie!

443. I'll end this no-limit section with another quote from World Champion Chris Ferguson, "Skill, talent, and some luck can get you the to the top, but it takes heart and discipline to keep you there." That right there is a ton of poker wisdom for you.

3.

Seven-Card Stud

Seven-card stud, limit hold'em, and no-limit hold'em are the three most popular poker games played publicly today. These three games are alike (they're all poker) but very different.

While researching the history of poker, I learned that during the Civil War soldiers played five-card draw, which has two rounds of betting. Wanting more action and another round of betting, the fellows developed a new poker game called stud poker. The game was named after the stud horses that often had to pull the heavy cannons and wagons out of the mire. I suppose the soldiers wanted to get their poker game out of the mire. It is said that during World War II, soldiers changed their nightly game of five-card stud to seven-card stud so they could have two more rounds of betting, which added the extra action they craved.

Many players cut their poker teeth on seven-card stud. Although less popular in Las Vegas than it was a decade ago, the game is still played in casinos, in poker tournaments, and on millions of kitchen tables across the nation. You can find hold'em games in any casino or card club that offers poker, but if you're looking specifically for seven-card stud you better make a phone call to be sure. Seven-card stud seems to be more popular on the East Coast than the West. Most casinos in Atlantic City offer stud from low limit to middle limit. Trump Taj Mahal offers a huge limit ($300-$600) on weekends. Low-limit games can be found daily in casinos in Arizona, Mississippi, Colorado, Washington, and Nevada. Foxwoods Casino in Connecticut offers seven-card stud with limits from $1-$2 for beginners all the way up to no-limit. No-limit seven-card stud is rare in America but popular in Europe. If you're extremely wealthy and want the challenge of seven-card stud, you'll need to take your private jet to Los Angeles for the $1,000-$2,000 game spread on the weekends at the Hustler Casino. Larry Flynt often plays in that game. It is rumored that Mr. Flynt built his casino so he could find a high-limit game of seven-card stud whenever he wanted.

To quote the 1982 Ladies Seven-card Stud World Champion of Poker, June Field, "The game of poker is like life…the amount of effort you put into it determines the rewards you'll receive from it. To succeed in life takes knowledge, experience, determination, and hard work. Yes, you'll make mistakes and meet with failures along the way, but these too serve a purpose. These same attributes apply to poker. Add healthy doses of patience, self-discipline, and a positive attitude and you'll have what it takes to be a winner in life and at poker. One more thing, the most important…skill."

Seven-card stud is definitely a game of skill and memory. It is not a flop game with community cards. To reiterate the basics: each player antes (very low limits often have no ante), then all players receive two cards down and one card up on the initial deal; this is followed by a round of betting. The lowest card opens the betting with the minimum bet (or the maximum) and the action rotates from there in a clockwise pattern. The fourth card is dealt faceup followed by a round of betting; this time the highest card opens the betting, but this player also has the option to check. Then comes the fifth card also faceup, a round of betting, the sixth card faceup and another round of betting, and then the last card, dealt facedown, followed by the last round of betting. After the last round of betting comes the showdown. The player holding the best five-card hand out of seven cards is the winner.

Seven-Card Stud Tips for the Beginner

444. In all flop games you will know what the nuts or second nuts can be. In seven-card stud, some hands can really surprise you because each player has three downcards; they literally could turn over quads (four-of-a-kind) at the showdown without showing a pair.

445. The first and most important point to study in stud is hand selection—which hands you will choose to play after the initial deal of three cards.

446. The best starting hand is rolled up trips. How sweet it is! But that doesn't happen too often. As a matter of fact the odds against it are 424-to-1.

447. The next best hand to start with is a high pair, followed by a medium pair with a high kicker. A baby pair is dangerous; enter the pot only if you have a big kicker. Small pairs with small kickers could lead to problems.

448. Three high cards to a suit is a fine hand if you don't see your suit or high cards all over the board. Beware of entering the pot with one high card to a suit and two low cards.

449. Example: 2♠-Q♠-4♠. This is a tempting but dangerous hand. If the pot isn't raised, it is okay to call and see the fourth card, provided you haven't seen a herd of spades on the board. If fourth street is not a club or a queen, let the hand go if it is bet. If you pair the deuce and continue, you could ultimately cost yourself money.

450. The reason this type of hand can cause problems is if you catch a two or a four. That sucks you into continuing the hand even if your clubs and queens are falling everywhere but in your hand. If this happens, fold unless it is checked to you and you can see a free card (which probably isn't going to help).

451. Many new players, or even players who have been playing stud for eons but have never taken the time to study the game, play any pair. They don't look around the board, they just know they have a pair, hold their nose, and jump in.

452. The reason players do this is because they have made bad plays in the past and ended up making a hand and winning the pot. To them, this is a green light to play badly.

453. As mentioned, the lowest card on the board starts the action. If there are two or three deuces on the board, the suits are ranked alphabetically—clubs, diamonds, hearts and spades—so the club would open. If there were no deuce of clubs then it would be the deuce of diamonds.

454. Keep this in mind: successful stud players look for a reason they should *not* enter a pot after the deal. Losing stud players look for any reason *to* stay and play.

455. Also, if a player enters more than 20 to 22 percent of the pots he is dealt in, he is either getting great hands and on a rush or he is ignoring starting hand criteria. The more hands a player plays, the worse he plays.

456. Other good starting hands are three to a straight (J-10-9) or three to a flush. Again, having at least one big card is important (4♥-7♥-A♥ rather than 3♥-4♥-7♥). The reason the big cards are important is that if your straight or flush doesn't come, you have an opportunity to pair a big card. To repeat, small pairs with small kickers can get you into trouble.

457. One of the best stud players I have ever known used to say, "If I make a straight or a flush it is because it just happened when I started the hand with a big pair. The only way I would take a fourth card to a straight or a flush is if I have all high cards and none of my cards are out. Pairs are what you want for starting hands in stud, big pairs."

458. The second most important decision is whether you will stay after the fifth card. The bet doubles on fifth street, making your hand selection critically important.

459. Let's get back to basics. Everyone will ante before the deal. Some very low-limit games have no ante, but as the limits go up there is always an ante.

460. After you receive your first three cards, two down (your secret) and one up, you decide if you want to play the hand. This decision, over the long haul, will determine whether or not you are a winning player.

461. You have an option of whether or not to play a hand unless you have the low card. This (and the antes) will be the only forced bet in stud.

462. When the fourth card is dealt, the high card then opens the betting. This player has the option also to check.

463. The bet on fourth street is the minimum unless the player has an open pair. He then has the option to bet the maximum. This is the only circumstance that the bet on fourth street can be the maximum and any player can make it the highest bet.

464. Example: In a $3-$6 limit game, three people decide to play after the deal. The low card was a 4, with one player showing a jack and another showing a 9. The fourth card paired the 4. That player can bet $3, $6, or check.

465. If he checks, either of the other two players can bet the $6; if he opens the betting with the lower bet of $3, either of his opponents can raise it to $9 (the $3 plus a $6 raise).

466. If the 4s checks and another player bets the $6, he then has the option of folding, calling, or if he was slow-playing three 4s, he could check-raise and make the bet $12. Remember, only when there is an open pair can the fourth street bet be the maximum.

467. When you play a hand, keep your cards in order. It is important for all players to keep their cards in the order they receive them.

468. As a matter of fact, it is incorrect for players to change the order in which they received their cards. If you have an opponent who rearranges his cards, call a floorperson if he continues. It is an unfair practice and a bad habit.

469. Why is it so important? An example: If you bring it in with the low card of a 4, and a 5 calls you, he may have split 5s. But, if on fourth he catches a deuce and places it as his door card, and then on fifth street he catches another 5, at a glance (if you didn't notice his door card in the beginning), you might not put him on three 5s. But if that 5 was where it belongs, where it was dealt, you should beware of the possibility of three-of-a-kind.

470. Many beginning players study their cards and the possible hands they could make, while looking only at their holdings. These people are not good players. Overall they will be losing players.

471. A good stud player will study the board if he is contemplating entering a pot. Only then will he make that decision.

472. Example: You have a 3♦ and Q♦ down and a 3♠ up. A deuce opens the betting. You do not automatically call because you have a pair.

473. You look around the board. If you see any 3s or queens your chances of catching another 3 or a queen have been reduced. If you see five diamonds on the board, your chances of making a flush have been reduced. However, unless you have three to a suit, you shouldn't even be considering trying to make a flush. But, you also should be aware of the number of diamonds that are out just in case you begin catching one diamond after another.

474. On the other hand, if the pot has not been raised and you see no 3s or queens, call the bet. Your next decision is whether to stay on fourth street. If you catch a 3, your baby pair just grew into a big hand. If you catch a queen you're looking pretty good with two pair.

475. If a card lower than a queen bets, you should raise if you have the two pair. If you have trips, you will want to slow-play (just call) until fifth street when the bet doubles.

476. Always think, "How can I get the most profit?" when you have a big hand. It's tricky. You don't want to slow-play and let them catch up, but you don't want to run them out of the pot either.

477. Remember: at low-limit stud, players usually have what they are representing. They seldom bluff. Example, if a player showing a king bets, he probably has a pair of kings. If a player catches a third club on fourth street and bets or raises, he probably has a flush draw.

478. One of the best lessons you can learn in the beginning is how to read the board. This takes much more concentration in stud than in hold'em.

479. You will need to remember what cards are out, not only in relation to your hand but also in relation to your opponent's hand. If you have a pair of 7s in the pocket with a 10 up, you need to immediately look around the table for 7s and 10s.

480. If you raised with your 10s and a jack reraised, you need to look around the board for jacks. If you see one, good. If you see two, better. You will know he cannot make a set.

481. You have to constantly be thinking and remembering. You need not only think about what you need to make your hand versus what cards you can see, but also what your opponent might be trying to make and what cards you can see that will help (or hurt) his hand.

482. I do not suggest going for a low straight or flush. If you are dealt a 2♦-5♦-7♦, let it go unless you are the low card bring-in, the pot is not raised, and you catch another diamond. If you have been paying attention and you haven't seen more than two diamonds, take the next card. If you have seen three or more, let it go.

483. The reason is that if you do pair, it will be a baby pair. Baby pairs, even two of them, are easily beaten. Why put yourself in that position?

484. The same holds true for a 6-5-4 on the deal. You would need a 3 or a 7 to continue if you want to go for a straight, but I do not recommend this. You may make a baby pair, but so what? It will almost always get you nothing but trouble.

485. When considering going for a straight in this situation, look around the board not only for the cards you will need, but also for any 5s or 10s. You cannot make a straight without a 5 or a 10 in your hand.

486. The exception: If you are dealt a 2♣-J♣-A♣. Now that's a whole new ball game. Look quickly around the board. If you see no jacks or aces and only one or two clubs, you have the possibility of making a big pair or a big flush.

487. If you are dealt a K-Q-J, again it is a whole new ballgame with much greater potential than the baby cards to a straight. Take a card on fourth street if you have not seen your cards sprinkled around the table. If you get help in any direction, a 10, a J, a Q, a K, or an ace, continue with the hand—if your cards are live.

488. If you are dealt a pair with one card up and one down, that is called a split pair. If you are dealt a pair with both cards down, this is called a pocket pair.

489. If you are dealt a split pair of 10s and a player with an 8 bets, you should raise (because you put him on a pair of 8s). If an ace raises, that's different; he could have split aces, so just call. You should know if there are any 8s or aces out, which will help you decide if you want to continue the hand.

490. When making the decision of whether or not to enter a pot or call a raise, ask yourself, "Is this a mistake?" If you can honestly answer, "No, this is correct," then go for it. Next card, do the same ritual. It will become second nature. You won't always be right, but it will pay off in the long run.

491. In stud as in any poker game, you can make mistakes or play badly and win. That is the luck factor. But if you want to be a consistent winner, you must play mistake-free or as close to mistake-free as possible.

492. Remember also that other players make mistakes. If you are at one end of a table with two big pair and your opponent is at the other end of the table and calls a straight or a flush at the showdown, do not muck your hand. If you cannot see his hand, ask to see it.

493. It is the dealer's responsibility to read all hands. Always turn your hand up. If your opponent has a four flush and mistakenly called a flush, the dealer cannot award the pot to the winner (you) unless you have a hand. To reiterate, do not toss your hand until you have seen a five-card hand that can beat yours, no matter what your opponent announces.

Seven-Card Stud Tips for the Intermediate Player

494. George Percy, a seven-card stud expert from the 1970s and '80s wrote a poker primer in 1979 called *Seven-Card Stud: The Waiting Game.* It was the primary source for the beginning study of seven-card stud for ten years. Stud is considered a waiting game because you really need to wait for good starting hands.

495. Stud is also called the memory game. If you have a photographic memory, seven-card stud is a great game for you!

496. As mentioned, one of the best lessons you can learn early on is how to read the board, but as you get more skilled at seven-card stud you will need knowledge of your opponents.

497. Once you figure out how your opponents play, you have a distinct advantage in the game. If you know a player is a rock, you should play only great big hands against him, and you also can often make him lay down the best hand.

498. Example: If you have pocket 3s with a king up and the rock is the only player to enter the pot and he has a queen (he very well may have two queens), you can raise. He will put you on split kings. If he doesn't help his queens by fifth street and you keep hammering, he will probably fold.

499. If your opponents are playing only their cards (that is, not paying attention to what is being dealt to other players) and playing only when they have a hand, you can do some ante stealing. Ante stealing is raising on third street with your goal being solely to steal the antes and the low-card bring-in money.

500. You do not necessarily have to have an opening hand to be a thief, although a big upcard is good to have for the visual effect. Most importantly you need position and heart. The thought on this is simply to stay a bit ahead of the game if you aren't getting any hands.

501. The higher the limit game you play, the more important ante stealing becomes. It is of course of no importance in low-limit games because there is no ante to steal. However, as you go up in limits, $15-$30, $20-$40, $30-$60, and so forth, the higher the limit, the more ante money is in the pot, often just waiting to be stolen.

502. Remember: poker is the one area in your life where lying and stealing are okay. In fact, these "traits" are not just okay; you must have them to be a winning player!

503. Example: You are playing a $15-$30 game where the ante is $2 and the bring-in is $5. Let's figure conservatively that thirty hands will be dealt in an hour. That is a cost to you of at least $60 an hour to play and that isn't adding in any $5 forced bring-in bets.

504. So we'll say it is costing you $75 an hour. If you win some hands, that's good. But if you add in some ante stealing, that's another $21 (eight players plus the low card that you can accumulate). Done three or four times an hour, this can really add up.

505. Example: You have a jack up and are the last to act. No one has entered the pot. Raise it and you can probably take it.

506. If you are in late position to act and can tell that the players that are going to act after you plan to fold, raise it and you can probably take it.

507. There will be exceptions to this of course; that's poker. Occasionally the low card bring-in will wake up with a big hand, but even if he calls, you could make a pair on fourth street. You can't get away with habitual ante stealing, but if you know how your opponents are playing, you'll have a good feeling of when you can do it.

508. You also can steal antes from experienced players. If you act after they do and they have folded, they simply can't stop you. When done correctly, ante stealing can be profitable.

509. As the levels increase, stealing antes becomes a very important strategy in a seven-card stud tournament. You must steal in order to stay alive.

510. If you have decided to steal the antes (and this should almost always be from late position), and you get raised, fold immediately if you don't have a hand. Cut your losses. As long as you win two out of three, you're fine.

511. Remember, you cannot steal if a player has already entered the pot. He came in with something. Just wait for a better opportunity.

512. Always have the idea to steal the antes in the back of your mind if you are last or late to act. This is especially true in seven-card stud tournaments. Get away with as much as you can.

513. In tournaments, you can steal from earlier positions if you have the highest card on the board. If an aggressive player is stealing a lot in front of you and not giving you the opportunity to be the "thief of the hand," wait for a marginal starting hand and then reraise him. Try to steal his steal. This is called a resteal.

514. Going after straights and flushes in live play is one thing. Pot odds and your outs will dictate whether or not you take the gamble. However, in stud tournaments stay away from those drawing hands if at all possible. You cannot replace those chips if you miss your draw. It could easily mean elimination from the competition.

515. Example: In live play if the bully raises every time he has the high card on board, wait for a small pair or three to a straight or three to a flush and then pop him back. He should back off, but if he calls and then checks to you on fourth street—you should bet it again.

516. The flip side of the bully coin is the passive, tight, weak player. Anytime he comes alive and jumps in with a raise you should fold unless you have a huge, made hand. It is unlikely that he would raise unless he had a big hand.

517. If you have to open with the low card and you have a big pocket pair, do not start pushing until fourth street. This will completely befuddle your opponents. Example: You have kings in the pocket but have to bring it in with a 3. There are two callers and a jack raises. Just call the raise as the others will probably do. Let's say you catch a 10 on fourth street. The jack bets, and then you raise. It will appear that the 10 helped your hand, making either two pair or three 10s. If the hand is played to the river, your kings will be a surprise.

Seven-Card Stud Tips for the Advanced Player

518. Staying focused is important in any poker game but staying focused and paying attention is extremely important in seven-card stud. Knowing what is going on and what cards are out is an important weapon in your arsenal.

519. Stud is very much a game of memory. You must try to remember what is on the board in relation to your own hand and in relation to others. Without a photographic memory, this is not easy but becomes easier with practice.

520. Example: You are dealt a 10, a jack, and a queen. You need a 9 or a king to make a four-straight. You also could pair any of your cards, so you need to look around the board quickly and make a mental note of how many of your needed cards are out. The cards you are looking for are 8s, 9s, 10s, jacks, queens, kings, and aces. If you catch a 9, you'll need to remember if the 8s are alive. If you catch a king, what is the status of aces? And of course, you could pair at any time, giving you another direction to take the hand.

521. You also need to remember cards that could help or hurt your opponent. Did a 7♦ catch a 3♦ and raise into a bunch of overcards on fourth street? If so, he may be going for a diamond flush. Have you noticed how many diamonds are out?

522. To be a winning poker player you must have confidence and trust your own judgment. As situations arise in various hands, analyze what you believe is happening, make a judgment, and do not second-guess yourself.

523. Example: You are dealt split 10s. A 3 opens the betting, you call, and a K♣ calls. He does not raise, so you don't put him on split kings. There are three other callers, so it is a five-way pot. You have a king with your 10s and on fourth street another king hits the board so you know he is not slow-playing rolled up kings. You catch a blank as does everyone else, but the K♣ catches a 3♣. An ace checks, you bet, the K-3 raises. You have not seen many clubs out so you immediately put him on a club flush draw.

524. He catches a blank on fifth street, as do you, but another player makes an open pair of 3s. The 3s check, as do you with your 10s, and the K-3 also checks. He raised on fourth street to try for a free draw on fifth street and it worked. He catches a club on fifth street and you catch a third 10. Now what?

525. You know he has a club flush. Everyone checks to him and he bets; now it's just you and him in the pot. Of course you go for a full house, but you don't fill up. This is where you listen to your original determination of his or her hand and fold your trips. Do not—I repeat *do not*—now try to talk yourself out of your original analogy of his hand. It's time to make one of those tough laydowns.

Remember the poker adage; money saved spends as well as money won.

526. I have suggested you start with good starting hands, but what do you do if you don't improve? Example: You start with split aces and you play them tough. By the river, you haven't even made a second pair. What do you do?

527. This is where knowing your player is so very important. First of all, check if a conservative player bets because he probably has you beat. On the other hand, if you are against only a skilled player who also has not improved his hand, a check-call would be in order.

528. At the opposite end of this scenario is the instance when you make a huge hand. How do you get the most profit from your opponent? It depends on many factors.

529. If you fill up on the river and have no pair showing, you are most likely in the lead. If you fill up and do have a pair showing, the best circumstance will be if your opponent had been drawing to a straight or a flush and made his hand.

530. If this is the case, whether or not you bet depends on how your opponent plays. If he is an inexperienced player, you may be able to get a check-raise out of him.

531. If he is experienced he may raise you, but he also will call a reraise with his flush or straight, just in case he believes you have two high pair or trips. He will want to believe that you have a hand that he can beat. You may even be able to induce a bluff bet from him if he missed his flush but believes you are a strong enough player to lay down two pair.

532. Bluffing is in the bag of tricks of any good poker player, the seven-card stud player included. You set up a bluff just as in a hold'em game. You begin by representing yourself as a solid player. You have raised or reraised with nothing but what you were representing for hours.

533. When the time is right and you have two small cards down and an ace or a king up, raise it. The time will be right if you are playing against no maniacs and you believe that the other players will fold.

534. You can occasionally get a weak player to fold the best hand. Don't try to get away with this too many times.

535. Example: You have a pair of 3s in the pocket and a jack up. A tight player enters the pot with a 10 for the minimum bet because he has a queen and your jack to act behind him. The queen folds, and you raise. Even if your tight opponent has a pair of split 10s, if he calls and checks on fourth street and you bet, in all likelihood he is going to fold.

536. Sometimes you might have to carry a bluff or a semibluff through fifth street. In doing so, you may even make a hand. However, if you bluff through fifth street and still have nothing, but a player is calling you, it is time to give up the bluff. He is in the pot with something. Just check and hope he checks and gives you a free card because if he bets, you need to fold.

537. There will be times to sacrifice chips in order to save chips. One of these times is a busted bluff.

538. Never, ever give a player a free card on fifth street when running a bluff. That is when the bet doubles and when he might decide it's time to give up because of the strength you are showing (you sly fox).

539. It is different being the bluffer or the bluffee. If you suspect someone is doing a lot of bluffing, do not chase him without some strength. The more he bluffs, the less strength you need—but attack aggressively. Don't be calling!

540. A good rule of thumb for bluffing is to bluff more at the tighter tables and bluff less at the looser tables. If you don't like your table, change tables!

541. If you're in a tournament, you do not have the option of changing tables. Sit tight; eventually your tournament table will break and you can start fresh at a new table. I have been in major tournaments and literally waited hours for a starting hand, surviving only on a few stolen antes here and there. But suddenly with a little rush and three or four winning hands, you can be way ahead of the game. You'll go from the outhouse to the penthouse in a period of fifteen or twenty minutes. Patience!

542. When a player bets or raises aggressively with a pair showing, give him credit for his play unless he is a total loose canon. Give him credit for at least two pair if not trips. Do not stay unless you have two pair that you think is higher than his two pair might be.

543. The exception to this rule is if you are on a straight or a flush draw and the cards you need are live. Take this into consideration: Go after straights and flushes in multiway pots. This increases your pot odds. Going after a drawing hand heads-up with only a small amount in the pot is not worth the risk.

544. It often is a good idea to semibluff-raise with a good draw rather than to just call. This is especially true if your board looks threatening (like high suited connectors). Example: You have a 2♦-7♣, down and your board show is A♦-J♦-Q♦. You do not have a made hand, but it looks like you could have a huge made hand.

545. The exception is if it is seventh street. Then you have waited too long and you do not have the out of a draw. You should have made the move on sixth street.

546. Keep in mind that seven-card stud takes constant concentration not only on your hand and the cards you need but also on the changing strengths of your opponents' hands. Example: You put your opponent on a small pair and you have a medium pair. If your opponent catches an ace and check-raises, he probably made aces-up.

547. From another aspect of playing winning poker: you can be a poker superstar but if you are not in an emotional state to play, you will not win. A quote from Daniel Negreanu, "You've got to realize that when you're doing poorly, it's often based on your mental state. If you're having trouble in your life, it's virtually impossible to do well at poker."

548. If you have a lot of money or have built a good-sized bankroll from playing seven-card stud and decide to venture to the higher limits, proceed cautiously. You will be tiptoeing through a minefield.

549. Keep this in mind: players in $50-$100 games are usually very sophisticated and they will do a lot more bluffing than in mid-range limit games. They often will try to use the power of their money versus the power of their cards, so be prepared.

550. If you are winning and comfortable in your mid-level games, I suggest you stay there. Step up only if you need that adrenaline rush, and can afford to pay for it.

551. There also is nothing wrong with stepping up limits, giving it a try, feeling uncomfortable, and stepping back down. The level you do the best in is called your comfort zone. If you are smart enough to recognize your comfort zone, you'll be a winning player.

552. For those who want that high-limit adrenaline rush but really can't afford it, play a poker tournament. You could end up playing $2,000-$4,000 and winning a lot of money for a relatively small investment.

553. You can be the best stud player in the world, but if you are not a good money manager both on and off the poker table, you eventually will have no money to manage. Some bad habits to avoid include gambling (sports, craps, slot machines, and so forth). You'll have easy access to these things at most casinos, but they're a good way to squander your hard-won poker earnings.

4.
Razz

Razz is far from being one of the most popular poker games in the world. As a matter of fact, you will hardly ever find the game of razz in casinos or in Internet poker emporiums. But some folks love it, so it is often played in home games or some games of dealer's choice. In dealer's choice, the deal rotates around the table (clockwise) and each player who has the deal calls the game. The dealer usually selects poker favorites such as limit and no-limit hold'em and seven-card stud, but it is possible in one round that you could end up playing seven or eight different games.

Razz is still played in some major poker tournaments that offer mixed games. As of this writing, razz was still on the agenda of the World Series of Poker, crowning a new world razz champion annually. Ironically, this makes razz a game that is by and large found at two extreme ends of the poker community, home games and world championships!

In the simplest definition, razz is the opposite of seven-card stud. In seven-card stud you are always trying to make the *best* five-card hand out of seven cards. In razz, you want to do the exact opposite; you try to make the *worst* five-card hand out of seven cards. The ante, the deal, the betting rounds, and the showdown are the same as seven-card stud.

Razz truly is one of the easiest poker games to learn. As with all poker games, learning the basics of razz is a piece of cake, but the nuances can be difficult to learn and mastering them is what will determine if you are a winning or a losing razz player.

If you're looking for a fun game to add to your poker repertoire, razz may be the one. I believe it's important that you know the basic principals of razz because it will help you grasp seven-card-stud high-low eight-or-better, which is a popular game that is something of a combination of seven-card stud and razz.

A Note about Low Hands

You already know what a good high hand is, but what about good low hands? The best low hand is a wheel or bicycle, which is 5,4,3,2,A (1). You always rank low hands from the highest card down—the lower the highest card is, the better. For example: 7,6,5,3,2 (a "seven low") would lose to 6,5,4,2,1 (a "six low"). It also would lose to 7,6,5,4,2. The 7,6,5,3 is lower than the 7,6,5,4 because the 3 card is lower than the 4 card. Get it? With practice, it becomes easy.

A good low hand would be a six low or a good seven low. Although an eight low can win the hand or half the hand in split games, don't go for an eight low, it can too easily be beaten.

Razz Tips for the Beginner

554. Your goal in razz is the opposite of your goal in seven-card stud. Rather than making the best high hand, you want to make the worst hand or the best low hand. Players who are running bad in stud will often try razz to see if their terrible hands will continue coming because if they do, those same hands will be of value to them in a razz game.

555. Going for low does not mean a low pair. A pair, even a pair of deuces, will seldom win in razz unless you are playing heads-up in a tournament or shorthanded.

556. An ace is always low. The wheel, 5-4-3-2-1(ace) is the best razz hand you can make. Straights and flushes do not impair the low card value.

557. What will most often win in razz is a six, seven, or eight low. Example: 6-5-3-2-1 (ace), or 7-6-5-4-2 or 8-7-5-3-1. There will be times that a 10 or a jack low will win but that isn't the type of hand you will be trying to make.

558. A wheel is also known as a bicycle. FYI: The Bicycle Casino in Bell Gardens is named after this perfect razz hand.

559. In razz you can make a baby straight flush, and even though that is a magnificent high hand in all forms of poker, it is also a terrific low hand for razz. That is an exception to the worst-hand-wins rule in razz.

560. In seven-card stud the lowest card opens the betting after the deal. In razz the highest card opens. A king is the highest since the ace is considered low (a 1, so to speak) in razz. On fourth, fifth, sixth streets and the river, the lowest hand starts the action, which is also the reverse from stud high.

561. If you are playing against a good player who stays in on fifth street after catching a brick (big card: 9 or above), he will have a low door card, a low card on fourth street, and you can bet he has two low hole cards. Example: He has a 3 for his door card, a 5 fourth-street card, and he catches a king on fifth street but calls a bet to see sixth street.

562. Watching the board is as important in razz as in seven-card stud. You should look for cards that you need or cards that could hurt (or help) your opponents.

563. Example: You are dealt 7-5-3. If one of your opponents catches a king, that's good because that hurt his hand, and if another opponent is dealt a 7, that's good for you too because that is one 7 that you don't have to worry about hitting and hurting your hand by giving you a pair. You do not want a pair of 7s or a pair of anything. You want low cards—the lower, the better.

564. If you are the one who catches a king or another brick and your opponents catch low, say good-bye and wait for the next hand. If you chase cards in razz, you will be a losing player.

565. Babies, babies, babies, that's what you want on the deal in razz. Do not consider an 8 a baby. As a matter of fact, if you are dealt 8, 7, and 6, as intriguing as it appears, if there are two or more players left to act after you and they are showing a sprinkling of aces, 2s, and 3s, again say good-bye and muck that adolescent hand.

566. However, if you have that 8 high on the deal and the players yet to act have bigger cards, it is okay to take fourth street; you might even consider raising if your 8 is down and you have a baby up. If you catch another baby that does not give you a pair, you should be in good shape to continue with the hand.

567. If you catch a brick on fourth you probably will be finished with this hand. Remember, going to fifth street is the decision time in a seven-card game because that is when the bet doubles. You should see the fifth card only if it is checked to you.

568. Warning: razz can be hazardous to your psychological well-being. If you are not patient—extremely patient—and even-tempered, don't play razz. It will seem as if you will catch babies over and over again through fourth street and then brick, banana, brick. It's enough to make you pull your hair out!

569. As Linda Johnson, the 1997 World Razz Champion says, "Whoever stays calmest, is the most patient, and goes on tilt the least will get the money in razz." So wait and watch and when those bananas and bricks come flying at you, just muck, take a deep breath, wait, and watch some more, and you can be a winning razz player.

Razz Tips for the Intermediate Player

570. Chasing in razz can be just as expensive (and as dumb) as chasing in stud. If you are playing an eight low and looking at two players, both with seven lows—don't chase. Wait for the next opportunity. Just as in any other poker game, money saved is as important to your bottom line as money won.

571. It is okay to call after the deal with a 8-7 low or even a 9-8 low provided your opponents are high, 10-9 or J-10 and so forth. Whether or not you call to see fourth street will depend on how the board looks in relation to your hand.

572. If you catch a baby on fourth—great! As a matter of fact, a four-card hand is so much better than a three-card hand in razz, as opposed to stud that fourth street becomes more important in razz than in stud. All the better if there are not a lot of the babies you need to complete your hand on the board.

573. Whereas you bluff or semibluff with high cards and pairs in stud, the scare cards in razz are the little cards. Again, bluff only if your opponent is bluffable.

574. Example: You are dealt an ace and a 3 down and a 4 up. Naturally, you call or maybe even raise the pot. On fourth street you pair your 3 but your board looks great with a 3 and a 4. You are against two other players and one catches a 10 and the other a king. Try a bluff; you didn't help your hand on fourth street but they *don't* know that. They didn't help their hands and you *do* know that.

575. While it is not unusual to see four, five, even six–way pots in stud, it is unusual in razz. Most often, razz hands are played two or three-way from third street on. The reason: when a big card hits, a good razz player releases.

576. Professor McEvoy says, "You never should play on third street with a bad card against more than one other player. If you set that idea in stone, you'll be far ahead of the game."

577. As is true in all poker games, know how your opponents play. It can win pots for you. In razz, if the high-card bring-in player almost always throws his hand away to a raise, remember that. Then, when opportunity knocks, open the door. Example: If you have a baby up, no one has entered the pot, and you are last to act against this particular high-card bring-in, by all means, raise.

578. Entering a pot with an 8 low is not a good idea unless your 8 is the lowest card on the board. Even then, it is better if your 8 is down.

579. Seldom will you call a raise with a high card. The exception is if a player is continually raising when you have a high card and you think he is stealing. In that case, you need two extremely low cards to defend. If you don't catch a low fourth street, say goodbye. If you do catch good, stick around for fifth street. If all goes well, by sixth street you may actually have a hand. At the very least you will slow the bully down when he is playing against you.

580. If you have a four-card seven made on fourth street, you probably will be going to the river with the hand. The exception would be if babies are falling all around and you are catching a bunch of bananas (big cards). If there is a lot of action, you may decide to wait for a better opportunity. This is especially true in razz tournaments where you cannot buy more chips.

581. If you have limped into a pot with an 8 down and two babies but you catch a banana on fourth street, it should be an easy decision to fold if your opponent caught good. It's an even easier decision if you're against two players and they both caught good.

582. Ante stealing is certainly a part of a razz game but be selective. Late position with two low cards (one being up, of course) is a good time to become a thief. Never try an ante steal with only one low card up (and two big cards in the hole). It is too dangerous. An exception to the rule is if everyone folds to your low card and the bring-in has a paint.

583. A rough eight is like 8-7-6-5-3 while a smooth eight is 8-4-3-2-1. If you make a smooth eight but have some concern that your opponent is making a seven low, don't bet on the river, just check and call.

Razz Tips for the Advanced Player

584. Don't just raise but reraise as well on third street if a low card raises and you have three very good low cards. The only exception is if the original raiser plays very tight.

585. Example: You have a 4 up, and a 3 raises. He could be bluffing and with a reraise you could win it then and there or you could be building the pot for yourself. If you are called, this reraise also will give you pot odds to go to fifth street if you catch a brick on fourth.

586. Some hands play themselves on fourth street. In other words, a fourth baby is easy to play—of course you see fifth street. However, a good razz player will know what cards can help or hinder his hand or his opponent's hand as well as his own. This must be taken into consideration when deciding whether or not to continue in a hand.

587. If you bet and are called on fourth street, assume your opponent has a good hand but not necessarily a great hand. However, if a rock calls, that is cause for concern depending on what fifth street brings you both.

588. There will be times that a good draw is better than a made hand. For example, if you believe your opponent has a 10-9 or a J-10 made hand and you have 5-4-3-2, your needed cards are live, but you catch a great big brick, this is a good time to go for the draw.

589. If you are playing well, you know how many of your cards are live. If it's a lot, go for it. When you catch, you're in the driver's seat. Although this situation is nerve wracking, you will make more money if you catch your needed card on the river. This will give your board a look of deception. Your opponent could help his hand but if you catch the perfect ace or 6 (maybe even a 7 will do it), you'll win a big pot.

590. If a good player enters a pot with a call or a raise, you can conclude that he has two smaller cards down. Example: He is showing a 7; you can bet he has two cards lower than a 7 down.

591. If you have a beautiful low draw against one opponent after fourth street but catch a brick on fifth street while he catches perfect, it is okay to take the fifth card. This scenario changes if you are against several players who also show improvement or if you have seen many of your needed cards hit the muck.

592. If you played a perfect draw to the river against one opponent only to end up with a nine low, it is okay to call if your opponent's board is non-threatening or if you believe he is bluffing. If your board looks dangerous (7-5-4-3), don't just call if he bets—you should raise! Don't give him a chance to "win by accident." This means if he has a 9-8 low, he may fold to a raise but if you just call his bet when he wouldn't have called your raise, at the showdown he will win the pot by accident.

Razz is a great game for a change of pace but like all poker games, patience is of utmost importance. If you want action, visit a craps table!

5.

Seven-Card Stud High-Low Split Eight-or-Better

Seven-card stud high-low split eight-or-better definitely holds the distinction of having the longest name for a game of poker. The shortcut names are simply stud split, stud eight-or-better, or stud eight. The game itself is sort of a combination of seven-card stud and razz; the highest hand wins half the pot and the lowest hand wins half the pot. The eight-or-better means that when playing for low, a player must make a low with an 8 or less. This is called a qualifier. There also is a game of seven-card stud split with no qualifier, which means that any low will win, as in razz. In eight-or-better the deal and the betting rounds are the same as stud or razz.

One player will win with the highest hand and one with the lowest. A player certainly can win both ways; that's called "scooping the pot" and this is the whole idea of this game. You always want to start out with the purpose of scooping the pot but it won't always work out. You will often make a high hand when you started in the direction of a low hand or a low when you started out headed for a high hand. It's sort of like getting lost on your way to a destination when you thought you knew the direction. You get totally misplaced but somehow you end up right where you wanted to be. You got there by an alternative route and everything worked out okay.

Eight-or-better is not available in many poker rooms in Vegas with the exception of higher limit games. One reason is that any split game is slower than non-split games; therefore, there are fewer hands dealt in an hour and the house makes less money. Generally, if poker rooms spread stud (short for seven-card stud high) about 25 percent of the time, they also will spread eight-or-better. You can find many lower limit, mid-limit, and high-limit eight-or-better games in California. In Washington, the Muckleshoot Casino offers $1-$4-$8 stud split; in Connecticut, Foxwoods offers limits from low to high; Bally's Park Place in Atlantic City offers a variety of limits; and the Apache Gold in San Carlos, Arizona, offers low-limit stud eight-or-better. To be sure, if you are looking strictly to play seven-card stud high-low split, you should call before making much of a trip and be specific. If they say, "Yes, we'll spread any game that is requested," be certain that the game you want is spread on a regular basis, not once every six months or only on weekends. It is a fun game to play at home, and you can find the game in many of the poker rooms on the Internet for practice.

Study and practice the following tips and become a winning seven-card stud high-low split eight-or-better player.

Stud Eight-or-Better Tips for the Beginner

593. If you are new to the game, you might think it sounds like fun simply because you can play more hands because you have two win opportunities. Wrong! If you play correctly, you probably will play fewer hands than in stud high.

594. As mentioned, your goal should be to scoop the pot every time you get involved in a hand. The way to do that is to start with three low cards that have the possibility of a low straight, a wheel, or a low flush. Scooper! (Most of the time.)

595. The object of this game is to win the whole pot every time, not just part of it. I call it my golden rule. Todd Brunson is the son of the world's poker guru, Doyle Brunson. I guess you might call him the Guru Jr. He has been winning poker championships since he turned twenty-one, and he is an expert seven-card stud eight-or-better player, so much so that his father had him write the chapter on the game in his book *Super Systems 2*. Todd calls the scooping concept the platinum rule.

596. Young Brunson advises, "When you are deciding whether or not to enter a pot or proceed to the next street, you should always ask yourself, 'Can I scoop this whole pot? Or am I playing for half?' If you are only playing for half, strongly consider folding."

597. When evaluating your hand, keep in mind that the value of a low hand is determined from the top, not the bottom. Example: An 8-7-5-2-A will lose to an 8-6-5-3-A. If you valued the hand from the bottom, the 2-A would beat the 3-A, but that isn't how it works. The 8-6 beats the 8-7. Get it?

598. The perfect low is 5-4-3-2-A. This will usually win both the high and the low but definitely the low. A perfect 6 is 6-4-3-2-A and a perfect 7 is 7-4-3-2-A.

599. Now your turn: Which is the better low hand? 8-7-3-2-A or 8-6-5-4-2? Again the 8-6 beats the 8-7 every time.

600. One more time: Which is the best low hand? 2-3-4-5-7 or A-2-4-6-7? The 7-5 beats the 7-6. Once you get it, you'll never even consider counting from the bottom.

601. Although eight-or-better resembles stud high in the way it is dealt and the betting rounds, they are not related—not even second cousins. You need to put stud high out of your mind as far as starting hand requirements are concerned.

602. In stud eight, the low card brings it in but on the remaining rounds the high hand acts first with either a check or a bet. So your first decision will be whether you will or you won't enter this pot. Ask yourself, "Do I have scoop potential?"

603. In a casino, cards speak. That means you do not have to declare if you are going high, low, or both. Simply turn your cards over and the dealer will read them and then either split the pot or push the whole thing to you (if you play the way I tell you to).

604. You absolutely can use the same card or cards to go high or low. Example: After seven cards you have 7-5-4-2-A-5-A. You have a low using the ace and the 5 and you have a high using the aces and the 5s.

605. You should be on the lookout for three small-connected cards (5-4-3), three baby flush cards (6♥-3♥-2♥) or three babies with a gap to a straight (5-3-2, or 7-5-4 and so forth). These are the ideal starting hands because they can so easily turn into a high (baby straight or baby flush) or a low.

606. As in stud or razz, study that board. What cards do you need to complete your hand? What does it look like your opponents need?

607. Do not play a big pair as you would in stud. Aces are the only exception, as aces with a baby is a good starting hand, especially split aces because your opponents won't know which way you are going and hopefully you'll win a scooper.

608. As your knowledge increases (and in tournament play), you can add queens and kings. But for now, consider them dangerous.

609. As a general rule, never enter a hand with thoughts of going high, especially with middle pair. Whether your kicker is a baby or a biggie, these hands are taboo. How can you possibly expect to scoop with a pair of 9s or 10s?

610. One exception on going high is with a rolled up hand. Your goal will still be to scoop the pot by putting pressure on the low draws and building the pot. Hopefully you'll either get rid of the drawing hands before the river or they will not make a low.

611. When you do have a big high hand and you are against what you believe to be a low, never assume and never stop raising. Many beginning players will just call a bet or even check because they are thinking the pot will be split when in fact their opponent had started for low, made two baby pair along the way, and didn't make the low at all. You're going to scoop so don't miss a bet.

612. Also if you believe you have the best low, especially if you have a low straight and you are against a low, bet or raise. He may have a good low but not as good as yours.

613. Seldom will you start with a high draw and end up with a low hand. That is why you don't start out to make a high hand. It is much easier for the low hand to end up qualifying for high than it is for the high hand to end up turning into a low.

614. Let's say you start with 5-3-A and end up catching a 2 and a 4 to make a wheel. It takes five cards to make a low hand; a high hand can win with ace high or any single pair. That is why you can easily "back into" a high hand when you started out with three pretty babies. You could have your low hand made in five or six cards and then pair, double pair, or even make trips to make a high also.

615. Each card can bring new possibilities or new disappointments. It can make you crazy when your first four cards are little bitty non-paired babies and then brick, brick, and brick. As you have to do when getting aces cracked in hold'em, take a deep breath and move on to the next hand. (You gotta have heart, miles and miles and miles of heart. I bet the fellow who wrote the song with that phrase was a poker player!)

616. Do not consider any three low cards playable. Don't even start with three lows if one is an 8. At best, this hand will be marginal; it loses to all other lows, except an 8. There are exceptions. (See Tips for the Intermediate.)

617. You may win some pots with an eight low, but that should happen accidentally. The problem with an 8 is that it is the worst low. You may make an eight low with an 8-7-4-2-A, only to be beaten by an 8-6 low (e.g., 8-6-4-3-A).

618. Now that you know what it takes to make low hands and how to read the board, you will know if you have made a low and your opponents are going high. In this case, raise until your socks melt. It is a sweet position to be in if you have two or three high hands battling it out, and you know you're going to get half the pot. Class dismissed.

Stud Eight-or-Better Tips for the Intermediate Player

619. Many inexperienced stud high-low players will play more hands than they should because they are lured to chase either end of that rainbow. You should look for reasons *not to enter* a pot. You will be winning money from those who find reasons to stay in a pot.

620. The single most important card in this game is an ace. Try not to enter a pot without one. As Professor Tom McEvoy, the 1983 World Champion says, "The ace in stud eight is like my American Express card. I try not to leave home without one."

621. Of course, nothing in poker is set in stone. You will enter many pots without an ace, but you should be doing so with babies. Examples: 4-3-2 and 5-3-2, and 6-4-3. These are fine, especially suited or even two-suited.

622. While the ace is the most important card to start with, the 5 is the second most important. Do you know why? Think about it. Why wouldn't it be a 2 since the goal is to start with three babies?

623. You must have a 5 to make a small straight or a wheel. Note: You cannot make any straight without a 5 or a 10 in your hand.

624. Your thinking has to do a reverse from stud high when you play eight-or-better. Unless you are in a stud high-low tournament, consider big pairs (that you would love to play in stud high) a dog of a hand unless they are aces, preferable with a baby.

625. The only time to consider playing a big pair—kings or queens—is from late position against a low draw. If you do, enter the pot with a raise. You would prefer to take it then and there.

626. If you start a hand with three babies and catch a fourth on fourth street that doesn't pair, you have almost an 80 percent chance of winning the low end of the hand—provided you have the lowest low. So go for the 6, maybe a 7, and almost always avoid 8s in your starting hands.

627. That is why with four low cards, especially if you have straight and flush possibilities, you want to build the pot. Just be sure your cards are live.

628. You will do less slow-playing in high-low than in regular stud. You will want to sandbag if you are rolled up or if you have three baby suited connectors and all of your cards are live. You want to encourage players, especially from early position, to put money in your pot.

629. If you help a rolled up hand, you need to play it in such a way that you have as many contributors as possible. This is a case where you want the low to make a straight or a flush. They will help you build the pot and you are almost assured half the pot.

630. Of course any rolled up hand or three or four suited babies can be beaten, but you want to maximize your win rate when you do have the opportunity. Those who don't maximize will win a lot of small pots and lose a lot of big ones.

631. If you decide to play a pot whether with a big hand or a nice baby hand, you should believe that you are going to win that pot. At the very least you should believe you will win half of the pot.

632. Remember, you should seldom enter a pot with an 8 in your hand. The exception to the rule is ace, deuce, 8 suited, and the cards needed to complete your hand are live. An ace, deuce, or an ace-3 suited with an offsuit 8 is okay. Again McEvoy says he will play that 8 all day long as long as he has a baby and that powerful ace. Stay in the hand only if fourth street helps you and remember banking on an eight low is usually unprofitable.

633. Another time you can consider playing an 8 is if you have connectors and a 5 with only one gap and your cards are live. Example: 8-6-5. Even more inviting would be an 8-6-5 that is suited.

634. You would not play this hand if your suit was everywhere and you saw a passel of 4s and 7s on the board. You must read the board, not only for your needed cards but for what your opponents might need.

635. Three big suited connectors is a tempting hand to enter the pot with. Examples: J♦-Q♦-K♦, or 10♠-J♠-Q♠. Do not yield to temptation. You have nothing. Remember: the idea is to scoop—that requires a low. (The only way you could scoop the pot with only a high hand is if the low doesn't get there, but you can't count on that happening.)

636. Looks can be deceiving, but most often you can tell whether a player is going high or low by his door card. By fourth street you should have an even better idea of the direction your opponent is going.

637. If you have split aces with a little card or a big buried pair with an ace up, always bring it in with a raise. This is the most confusing hand you can have in the eyes of your opponents. They don't know if you're raising on a high or a low.

638. If a queen or a king has raised before you, reraise. This may run low draws out.

639. It is easy to call a double raise if you think you have the only low draw and you have gobs of outs, but if it is an ace doing the reraising, you should fold. If you don't, you are playing badly.

640. It is okay to enter an unraised pot with a baby pair and a baby kicker. Example: 2-4-2. Amazingly, unlike in stud high, a baby pair or two pair will win the high end many times. Of course your goal is always to scoop.

641. If you make two baby pair, be careful unless your two pair are aces-up. It will take trips, a straight, or a flush to beat you. Watch the board and put your opponents on hands when deciding whether or not to proceed.

642. Remember, fifth street is decision time. If you call on fifth street you need a good hand or a great draw and your cards should be live. Fifth street is when the bet doubles and to continue is to commit yourself to the pot.

643. The inevitable exception to the rule is if you catch bad on sixth and your opponents catch good. Then it might be time to rethink that commitment.

644. In the beginners section I mention playing one-gapper starting hands. As you advance and know how to read the board and the other players, it is sometimes okay to enter the pot with a two-gapper if your needed cards are live. Example: 6-3-2 or 7-4-3. You must improve on fourth street to continue.

645. If you are lucky enough to start out with a great low draw like 3-2-A, or 4-3-2 suited and you see none of your needed cards, play this hand aggressively from the get go. You're actually betting on the come but the odds are with you. Just in case you make a low but someone has a high and you have to split the pot, you want a decent pot to split.

646. It is okay to play a big pair with a big kicker against players who obviously are going low—but only if an ace is not looking back at you from their hands. These types of hands can be trouble so proceed with caution.

647. With your goal always being to scoop, if you do decide to play a big pair against low draws, do so aggressively. Make the players who are going for low pay a big price to see all the cards. More often than not, if you are against good players, they will fold sooner rather than later (especially in tournament play). If they do stick around, be on the lookout for little straights and flushes. Ideally, one opponent will pick up a small pair to encourage him to continue with the hand at about the same time you trip up or double pair.

648. Avoid getting caught in the middle but try to trap other players there if you can. Example: You enter the pot with a 4-3-2. You catch a jack on fourth and a low behind you bets or raises. Let it go and wait.

649. Try to trap the players going low with your great hands. If you believe you have the best low made, raise until the sun burns out. Example, you made an 6-4-3-2-A on fifth and your opponent is showing a 7 and raising. He may have a 7-5 made or a 7-4 but you are leading the pack with your 6-4. You need to feel confident that he hasn't made a straight. That confidence should come if you know that his straight cards are dead.

650. There will also be times to allow yourself to be trapped. Actually, you will only appear to be trapped when really you are holding a monster hand. Example: You have kings in the pocket with a deuce up and you have to bring it in. Four players limp in and you catch a king on fourth. A queen bets and two lows call. Just call. If you fill up on fifth, continue to slow-play. If you don't make a full house, throw it into high gear on fifth when the bet doubles. The dream scenario is if you fill up on fifth, the queen appears to be a flush or a flush draw and one of the lows looks straight. Now you're in the driver's seat for sure. Sit back and enjoy the ride. Don't raise until the river. This type of situation can make your session—especially if the low doesn't get there.

651. The only time to proceed to fifth street if you started with a beautiful low and caught a banana on fourth is if there is no raise and your cards are live. Normally, three babies and a brick means good-bye for this hand.

652. The exception is three babies and a brick, four-suited. If you haven't seen your suit all over the place, you'll want to continue with the hand. If you make four babies and a four-flush, even with a brick, plan to take the path that leads to the river. You have great potential for a scooper—provided of course your needed cards are live.

653. If you decide to take sixth street, you should have at least four babies. If you're headed low or if you have decided to take the high road, you should have at least two pair, trips, or a four-flush. Three-of-a-kind should have you way out front on the high end and you have the potential of filling up if you need to.

654. Another fifth street concept: If you have a made hand on fifth, whether high or low, don't raise. You don't want to lose any customers that want to give you money.

655. If it is checked to you on fifth and you have your made hand, you may even want to check along. Another McEvoy quote, "The stronger your made hand on fifth street, the slower you should play it."

656. And another: "The weaker my opponents, the more likely I am to check in order to trap them. The more sophisticated my opponents, the more likely I am to bet to make them pay to try to draw out on me." (If you are wondering why I quote Professor McEvoy so much, it is because he was one of my very first poker teachers and a very good one. I owe a lot of my success to this one man.)

657. Get the most bang for your buck when you make a nice low straight. If you are against what appears to be one or two high hands, and perhaps another low draw, just check. Don't raise—yet.

658. Usually in a seven-card game the decision of whether or not you will continue is made on fifth street when the bet doubles. In stud eight it is not so taboo to fold on sixth street if you haven't sufficiently improved. Example: You started with 2♥-3♥-5♣, a strong low. You caught a 6♥ on fourth. Looking good but now you are seeing a lot of your needed cards out. You take the fifth street card, hoping for an ace, a 7, or a heart. Then boom, boom you catch brick, brick on fifth and sixth. This is one of those times you should fold on sixth. Sad but true.

659. As right as it is to build a pot when you know you have a winner and to slow-play with a monster, you also need to save bets when you can. Example: You have two pair for high against only a low. If his low cards look as if he could make a straight, a check-call is the correct play. Save a bet when you can.

660. Bluffing is certainly part of this game. If you are last to act and you have a high card, take it away. You will bluff less in stud eight than stud high, but it is a tool of the trade.

661. Another good bluffing opportunity is when you have an ace up with middle cards behind you. Of course, as is true in any poker game, you can't bluff bad players. Your opponents have to at least be good enough to know that in stud eight they shouldn't play any middle cards.

662. Use deception to your advantage. Example: You enter the pot with a 2, and you have two 5s in the pocket. A queen raises, a 7 calls, and you decide to take one card because your cards are live. Let's say you catch an ace. The bet is on you, you check, the queen bets, the 7 caught an 8 and calls; now you raise. This is a semi-bluff, but you might eliminate the queens because he will probably think you paired aces, and you might get rid of the rough low because he thinks you're lower.

663. Now let's get complicated. If there is a loose, aggressive player who you believe is stealing a bit too much, wait for the right opportunity and try a resteal. Example: The low card opens and you are in late position with a hand that generally requires you to call. If the thief raises with a jack, don't just call him, raise him. If he calls but checks to you on fourth street, bet again. If he bets on fourth and you still believe he's just trying to push you around, raise again. When the smoke clears you could either make a hand or get him to fold along the way. At the very least, you will slow him down.

664. Stud high-low split eight-or-better is a thinking (wo)man's game. If you want to drink and socialize, play low-limit hold'em.

6.
Omaha

I can't say for sure whether the game of Omaha originated in Omaha, but I'll take a good guess that whoever developed the game is an action addict. Even though you will have much more action in a game of Omaha than hold'em, you'll get even more in Omaha high-low, which I'll discuss in the next chapter. For now, the subject is straight Omaha high.

Omaha is a flop game in which you are dealt four hole cards. The flop, the turn, and the river are played the same as in any hold'em game as is the betting pattern. A round of betting follows the deal, the flop, the turn, and the river, and then comes the showdown. The big difference between Omaha and hold'em is that you have a lot more combinations with which to make your best five-card hand than you do in hold'em. In hold'em you have seven cards to work with and in Omaha you have nine cards to make your best five-card hand. You *must* use two cards out of your hand to make your best possible high hand. If you believe you are a good hold'em player do not think you automatically will be a good Omaha player just because you have more ways to make a hand. The strategy is very different. The game is much more volatile than hold'em. True Omaha players love to see an experienced hold'em player arrive in their game for the first time. Hold'em players often see Omaha as sort of double hold'em because they have four cards to work with rather than two. Not! Study the following tips before your maiden voyage into Omaha territory. Otherwise, you will spend a lot of money (which will make a lot of your new Omaha friends very happy) while you discover just how different the games are. The first big disappointment in Omaha is that if you flop the nuts, they seldom will remain the nuts. That can get very frustrating, but it's just the beginning.

665. You will discover that there is more preflop raising in Omaha than in hold'em. If you generally would buy into a low-limit hold'em game with $100, allow $200 in the same limit Omaha game. You need more investment to play, but your wins will be greater because it is such an action-filled game.

666. You will notice many players getting into action almost every hand. You must have the self-control to be conservative in your hand selection. Wait on good solid starting hands.

667. Many hands are unplayable. Example: Do not play if you pick up trips, even aces. You would love to flop trips but you don't want to play with three of a kind in your hand. This reduces your chances of flopping trips by 50 percent. Consider this hand a no-go-so-fold. If trips are a no-go-so-fold, picking up quads is a double no-go-so-fold faster.

668. Other hands to avoid in Omaha high are little straight draws and little flush draws. Example: 8-6-5-3, unsuited or 7♦-5♦-4♠-2♠. These types of hands will be high risk with low profit, so don't even get involved.

669. Do not continue on a flush draw if there is a pair on board. Full houses are too likely. Example: You hold ace, 3 of hearts, and an offsuit king and queen. The flop is 10♥-6♥-10♠. Fold and wait for the next hand if the hand is bet to you. Think about it. If the turn brings a jack♥, yes, you have that beautiful nut flush. But what good is it if someone is holding a 10 and a jack?

670. Now for the hands you can and should play. Always play four cards that can work together to make your hand. Example: A♦-J♦-Q♠-10♠. This example is a hand that is double-suited, which makes it even stronger (pre-flop).

671. Another example of a double-suited hand is A-10 suited with A-K suited. This gives you a lot of outs for big hands; trip aces or a full house, the nut straight, the nut flush, even straight flushes and royals are possibilities.

672. Other good starting hands are high double pairs. Examples: A-A-K-K (raise preflop); K-K-Q-Q (raise from late position or call a raise from any position); A-A-Q-Q (raise preflop or call all raises); K-K-J-J (raise or call raises); Q-Q-10-10 (raise preflop from late position or call a raise from any position). Any combination of high pairs is worth paying to see the flop. Being double-suited adds strength to these hands. These examples have good potential for high straights, flushes, trips, or full houses. These types of Omaha starting hands make your heart smile, but be sure to keep a poker face.

673. Lesser pairs such as J-J-10-10, Q-Q-9-9, or 10-10-8-8 come further down on the preference list but are okay hands with which to see an unraised flop. Coming down the starting hand ladder another rung are hands such as 9-9-8-8, 8-8-7-7, or J-J-8-8. These could flop playable hands, but they could just as easily flop trouble hands. Enter the pot only from late position and with no raise with such hands.

674. The hands that will win the most money in Omaha are straights and flushes. However, do not draw to these hands unless you are drawing to the nut straight or flush and there is no pair on the board.

675. When drawing to a straight, try to have a "wraparound" hand. Example: Q-J-10-9 or K-Q-J-10. Wraparound hands are hands that can make a straight from either end. Example: With A-K-Q-J, only a 10 can make a straight, but with K-Q-J-10, a 9 or an ace will make the straight—that's a wrap!

676. Two of the best starting hands in Omaha are A-A-K-K, double-suited and A-A-J-10, double-suited. Being double-suited adds nut flush draw strength. Being single-suited is okay too. Any of these starting hands are worth a preflop raise. If you are not single or double-suited with these hands, just call before the flop.

677. High cards are preferable but not necessary. Small cards that are four connectors (wraparound hands) or that are connectors with a pair are okay. Example: 7-6-5-4, or 10-9-8-7, or 8-7-7-6, or 9-9-8-7.

678. When playing these small or middle cards that work together, don't even think about being suited. What are you going to do if you flop an 8- or 9-high flush? No, you're looking for sets, full houses, or nut straights.

679. Remember Omaha is a game full of busted hands and disappointments, so patience and perseverance are an absolute part of your game plan if you are to be successful. Also keep in mind that when you do make a hand stand up, you usually will win a big pot because of all the action.

Omaha Tips for the Intermediate Player

680. Omaha is a game where you want to be going after the nut hand, not the second nuts, especially in low-limit. Why? Because in low-limit most players want to see the flop; therefore most hands are multiway and all the action builds the big pots! In multiway pots, the nut hand is going to show up and win most of the time.

681. Many new Omaha players will play too loosely. They will occasionally make a hand with loose calls, but overall, their win rate will be disastrous. As is true for the winning player in any poker game, be wise when making your hand selection.

682. Notice if a player is looking at the board and back and forth to his hand. This most likely indicates a straight or a straight draw.

683. Stay away from the small and middle pairs. Sets don't win very often and even if you flop a set, someone may have flopped a bigger set.

684. Playing big pairs is different. Example: K-K-Q-Q is a good starting hand because you have big set or full house possibilities. Additionally, you have straight possibilities.

685. To reiterate, J-Q-K-A is a good starting hand, especially if you are double-suited. However, ace-little suited is not such a good hand in Omaha high because you are limiting yourself to the nut flush draw.

686. Consider this: your hand needs to be coordinated. Example: A-J-A-10, double-suited. This type of hand gives you a lot of outs (a straight, a flush, or a full house, for example) and the more outs you have the stronger your hand is.

687. Small coordinated cards are playable in multiway unraised pots. Examples: 6-6-5-4, or 7-7-6-5. If you do not hit immediately, let it go like the cards are on fire!

688. Likewise, hands such as 10-9-8-7 or 6-5-4-3 are playable from late position. Again, if you don't catch a perfect flop or draw to the nuts, the hand is too hot to hold on to, so dump it!

689. Do not draw to a straight if there are flush cards on the board. Example: You hold A-K-J-10, rainbow. The flop comes 9♠- 8♠- 3♠. Even though you hold an open-ended straight draw, if there is a flush possibility, someone most likely will have the spades.

690. Do not draw to a straight or a flush if the flop brings any pair. If you make a straight or a flush, somebody easily could have you beat with a full house.

691. If you flop the nuts and a scare card comes on the turn, proceed cautiously. If you find yourself in the middle of a raising war, let it go, as you are most likely beat. Example: You hold A♠-K♥-Q♦-10♠. The flop brings J♠-7♠-2♠. Beautiful, you have flopped the nut flush. However, if the turn brings the J♣ and it is bet and raised before the action gets to you, it's time to take a deep breath and muck your hand because your beautiful nut flush just turned to dust.

692. Among his many other titles, Tom McEvoy is the 1992 Omaha High World Champion. He says about the game, "Omaha high can be brutal! It's a cold, cruel world and it's a cold, cruel game." (But it's not as cold and cruel as Omaha split, which is even more aggravating!)

693. Your disappointment and aggravation are soon forgotten when you flop the nuts but hold your breath for the turn and the river and hope that no scare cards come. If you have bet the hand, as you should have, you will rake in a nice-sized pot. All your enemies who were drawing at their hands either drop out or call your bet with the second-best hand and you win this one!

694. Raising hands in Omaha high such as A-K-Q-J, single or double-suited, are preferable to a big pair with connectors like Q-Q-J-10. If you're in late position, you may even want to put in a raise or a reraise with these hands.

Omaha Tips for the Advanced Player

695. If you know that a player raises with aces and paints or aces double-suited only, and another player with the same criteria enters the pot, you may want to call that raise with middle cards because you know where the aces are. If you call with a hand like 7-6-5-4 or 7-7-5-4, and flop a set or a small straight, you'll probably snap those aces right off.

696. Flopping top two pair in Omaha, and sometimes only top pair when against just one opponent, is often a good hand (top two is of course, better). However, if there is action before you, be very cautious if you flop bottom pair or even bottom two pair.

697. Be prepared to dump bottom set whether playing against one opponent or a whole herd of opposition. Remember, there are a lot more sets made during one hand of Omaha than in other games.

698. You should be bluffing less in Omaha than the hold'em venues. However, if you are last to act and you enter the pot and flop top pair, and then a higher card comes on the turn but it is checked to you, bet. If any straight or flush possibilities died on the river and it is checked to you again, bet it again, but only against one or maybe two players. Don't even consider bluffing against three or more players. McEvoy calls such a foolish move "Omaha suicide."

699. T. J. Cloutier, a world champion Omaha player and author (in conjunction with Tom McEvoy) of *Championship Omaha* coined the word "dangler." It means a card that is of no use to your hand. Example: If you are holding K-J-10-4, the four is a dangler. The other three cards can work together to make a straight but the four is useless, the dangler. Even if that four is suited to the king, you don't want to be drawing to the second nuts.

700. T. J. advises, "Always play four cards that work together. Try to avoid having even one dangler." He calls it "the danger of the dangler."

701. You want to see your opponents entering pots with their danglers. They may try to slip in with such hands, but as McEvoy says, then they slip right out of the game busted.

702. Position is less important in Omaha high than in hold'em because there are so many more playable hands. Forget about stealing the blinds. This is just not part of the strategy of a good Omaha player because most of the time you will have a showdown.

703. When you hit a flop with top set, a nut straight, or flush, your question to yourself should be, "How do I maximize my profit?" Bet it out unless you are absolutely certain one of your opponents will bet it if you check it to him—and then check-raise.

704. Seldom will you check a big hand in Omaha because your opponents will probably call since Omaha is such a drawing game. Another exception is if you flop a monster like quads. Then you want to check or check and call and try to let your opponents catch up a bit in order to maximize your profit.

705. Omaha is an action game. Have the self-control to wait for premium starting hands and then if they fit the flop, play them aggressively. You also must have the self-control to muck a good starting hand before the turn card if the flop doesn't help your hand. If you can follow these guidelines you will be a winning Omaha player.

7.

Omaha High-Low Split Eight-or-Better

If Omaha is not fast-paced or action-filled enough for you, you may enjoy the rip roaring pace of Omaha high-low split. I suggested you fasten your seatbelt when you enter a game of Omaha high. If you want to join the Omaha high-low thrill ride, I suggest you buckle up, use a double harness shoulder strap, and have a roll bar!

"Omaha high-low was invented by a sadist and is played by masochists," is the way Shane Smith humorously described the game. I guess this description originated because of the horrible bad beats that you must endure when playing Omaha high-low. Of course, if you become an Omaha high-low player, you also will be distributing the bad beats on a regular basis.

One of the addictive factors of playing Omaha high-low eight-or-better, also known as Omaha high-low, Omaha eight, and eight-or-better, are the humongous pots that are more unusual than usual in a game of low-limit poker. The pots can get so big that you can literally take five or six beats in a row, scoop one pot, and be back to even if not winners.

As in Omaha, each player receives four cards from the dealer. As you find in hold'em and Omaha, there is a flop, the turn, and the river with betting rounds after the initial deal, the flop, the fourth card, and the fifth card, followed by the showdown. This is the point where the fun begins. You can use two cards out of your hand to make a high hand and two cards out of your hand to make a low hand. You *must* use two cards out of your hand and three board cards when going either way. (You cannot use four board cards or play the board.) However, you can use the same card to go one way or another. Example: You may use an ace for your high hand and then use that same ace again for the low, as long as you use another card in your hand to go with it.

Omaha high-low is no different from Omaha in that experienced players love to see the novice enter their game. They may be ever so nice and polite, but they are licking their chops and waiting for the kill. If you believe that your experience in stud high-low split has prepared you for the low end of Omaha high-low and that your hold'em practice has you ready for the high end, you are ever so wrong. Don't be the fish; be the fisherman. Read and study the following tips and prepare yourself for an emotional roller coaster before entering the murky waters in the raging sea of Omaha high-low split. You might get aggravated. You might win the biggest pot in your poker career. One thing is for sure—you won't get bored!

Omaha High-Low Tips for the Beginner

706. The single most important tip to remember about playing Omaha high-low is that it is a game of the nuts. The second nuts is a terrific hand in a lot of poker games, but not this one!

707. You will be playing for the best high hand and the best low hand. As with seven-card stud eight-or-better your goal is to scoop the pot. You want to play hands that have high and low possibilities or high possibilities when the low does not get there.

708. You will have two important decisions to make with each deal—whether or not to play the hand before the flop and then whether or not to continue after the flop. Making the correct decisions will determine whether you will be a winning player or a contributing player. Keep reading for the criteria for these decisions.

709. Remember, you must use two cards out of your hand and three cards on the board to make your best five-card hand. You want all four of your cards to be able to work together. Example 3-2-A-A double-suited such as 2♣-A♣-3♥-A♥.

710. Raise and reraise with the nut high hand but do not raise or reraise with the nut low in a multiway pot because you could get quartered. This means that if you hold the 2-A and that is the nut low and another player holds another 2-A, you both win half of the low end of the pot, which equals one quarter of the total pot. With the nut low, you will be better off just checking and calling. By being quartered you literally can lose money even though you win part of the pot. There's a story about an Omaha high-low player who kept making the nut low and stated, "If I keep winning with my ace-deuces, I'll go broke!" This is a player who is being "quartered to death."

711. World-class poker player Barbara Enright has said, "The sweetest two words I love to say in a game of Omaha high-low at the showdown is, 'Nut-nut.'" Nut-nut means the nut high and the nut low. Even if a player is quartered on the low of a nut-nut hand, he will win three-fourths of the pot.

712. In Omaha high-low, if three of your four cards are 5 through 9, let the hand go! Do not play three middle cards, whether connectors or pairs.

713. As in Omaha high, the small and middle pairs can be trouble hands. Sets don't win very often and even if you flop a set, someone probably has flopped a bigger set or a full house.

714. Always look for reasons not to play a hand rather than looking for any excuse to play a hand. Playing too many hands is the biggest mistake beginner Omaha eight players make.

715. Shane Smith, Omaha high-low expert and author of *Omaha Hi-Lo Poker (Eight or Better) How to Win at the Lower Limits* preaches, "If it's possible, it's probable!" If it's possible for someone to have a higher high or a lower low than you do, it is probable that he does. The moral? Play or draw to the nuts only.

716. Smith also stresses the "Fit or Fold" rule. When your hand doesn't fit the flop, fold. This is your cardinal rule: No matter how pretty your starting hand is—fit or fold. If you hold clubs and diamonds come, fold—it doesn't fit. If you hold high cards and low cards come, it doesn't fit, so fold!

717. The second biggest mistake beginner Omaha eight players make is falling in love with their preflop hands and continuing to play them when they shouldn't. If you play correctly and patiently, you will be dealt another beautiful four-card combination that will fit the flop.

718. When going low remember that your highest low card, as in stud high-low, rates your hand. Example: 8-6-4-3-A will lose to 7-6-5-2-A. The 7-6 is lower than the 8-6.

719. Another nerve-wracking, hand-wringing, head-banging situation you will run into when playing Omaha high-low is being counterfeited. Example: You have an A-3 suited and a K-J suited in your hand, and the flop brings 8, 6, 2. You have the nut low. A beautiful sight…unless the turn or the river brings a 3. Because you must use two cards out of your hand, your nut low just went down the toilet.

720. Keep in mind, if the flop brings three cards higher than 8 (example: Q-J-9 or K-J-10), there can be no low. Therefore a high hand will be scooping the pot. If that is you, play the hand aggressively unless there are fewer than four players. With fewer than four players you don't want to lose a customer, so call if it is bet to you or bet if it is checked, but don't raise or reraise until the river (and then only if your nuts are still the nuts).

721. Also note that straights and flushes do not count against a low hand. Example: If you hold the ace and deuce of clubs and the board is 3♣-K♦-7♣-6♣-10♦, you have the nut low with the 7-6-3-2-A and the nut high with an ace-high club flush. Nut-nut!

722. An ace is the most important card in this game. It will serve the beginning player well to not play a hand without one. *Super Systems 2* refers to the ace as the "top of the food chain" in Omaha high-low.

723. Double or single-suited aces with small cards are great starting hands. Examples: A♠-A♦-2♠-3♦, and A♦-A♣-2♠-4♦. Hands such as these also help you to avoid getting counterfeited when going low, and they both have low straight possibilities in addition to nut flush possibilities. (As beautiful as these starting hands are, remember: if the flop doesn't fit, fold!)

724. If the flop brings only one low card when you are holding babies do not stick around for the turn. Chasing a low with a two-high-card flop is an absolute no-no.

725. Hands such as A-A-2-K and A-2-3-K are also good starting hands. They become more valuable if suited or double-suited. These types of hands give you high and low possibilities.

726. The advantage in Omaha high-low is that there is a lot of action, creating big pots. The disadvantage is that you can have the biggest nut-nut draw on the flop, miss it on the turn, miss it on the river, and your scrumptious "top of the food chain" starting hand needs to go down the garbage disposal. If you can't handle the heat, stay out of the kitchen!

727. Reading Omaha high-low hands takes practice. No other poker game has more misread hands at the showdown (even by some dealers). Before playing, try this: deal out six four-card hands and five board cards. Read the best high and the best low for all hands. Shuffle, deal, and repeat. When you can see the best high and the best low in each hand within about five seconds, you're ready for the Omaha high-low battlefield.

728. Your goal, of course, is to scoop the pot when you play a hand. Keep this in mind; a player who has decided to go both ways after the deal does not win most pots that are scooped. The scoopers will come either by a little ol' wheel or by a high hand when the low does not get there. Make sure this tip is burned into your mind and select your starting hands accordingly.

729. All Omaha eight experts are adamant about staying away from middle cards—5s through 9s. Example: You hold 8-7-6-5. Yes, you may flop a straight or a straight draw but know this, for this straight to be possible, there are also low possibilities: which means that if you play such cards and make your hand, you will win only half the pot. (Remember the goal…scooper!) Terrible odds if you intend to become a winning Omaha eight player, therefore consider such hands taboo.

730. Most of the time it takes the nuts to win in Omaha high-low. To reiterate, always draw to the nuts, particularly in low-limit games. The exception to the rule occurs as you go higher in the limits you play, or if you play Omaha eight tournaments (in the late stages of the event); you often will find a game where there are fewer people involved in every pot simply because of the cost to play. In this situation it won't always take a nut or a nut-nut hand to win. You will need to adjust to the texture of the game, the limit you have chosen, and how your opponents are playing.

731. In theory, you will see looser play before the flop in lower limit games, but you should play tighter after the flop. In higher-limit games usually you should play tighter before the flop and loosen up after the flop. Your solid, waiting-on-the-proper-starting-hands strategy does not change; you are changing according to how your opponents are playing. More often than not they are looser in low-limit and more solid in higher limit. You have to make a judgment call and play accordingly. I have heard of $100-$200 limit games being as loose as $1-$2 games, but not often.

732. Keep in mind that scooping the pot is the goal. An ace with two or three babies is a great starting hand because of the little straight possibilities in addition to the low hand value. An ace with two babies and a paint is also good because then you can go low and high.

733. There is an adage in hold'em: "If you study long, you study wrong." Carry this thought over into your Omaha high-low starting hands. If you are uncertain and have to contemplate whether to play your hand or fold before the flop, it's best to just fold.

734. Many times a hold'em hand will win without improvement. Example: aces, queens, and kings will often win with no board help. In Omaha eight-or-better, hands almost always need to improve to win.

735. This statistic does not mean you shouldn't raise before the flop. As a matter of fact, you should raise with your premium starting hands so that when you do hit, you win a bigger pot.

736. Playing high-only hands is okay if you can enter an unraised multiway pot and be ready to jump ship if the flop does not help your hand. Examples: A-K-J-J, or K-J-Q-Q, or wraparound hands like K-Q-J-10, or a wrap with one gap like A-Q-J-10; you get the picture. The flop will determine if your holdings are beautiful or so ugly it hurts your eyes.

737. Speaking of wraps, beware the baby wraparounds. Example: 5-4-3-2, or 6-5-4-3. This type of hand will most often trap you rather than send the pot your direction. It is best to avoid such hands unless you are in a late position in an unraised pot.

738. Playing big cards with pairs is an acceptable approach (preferably from late position with no raise) but playing three big cards with one dangler (a card that doesn't coordinate with the rest of your cards) is unacceptable. Example: K-K-J-Q or Q-Q-J-10 are okay but playing K-K-Q-7 or Q-Q-J-6 is not.

739. If the flop brings three cards higher than an 8, consider that the game just changed to Omaha high because there will be no low. If the flop brings two high cards that fit your hand, you need to bet or raise to try to chase out the backdoor low draws (players who will gamble with a low draw when only one low card comes on the flop). Do not give them a free card!

740. You should seldom if ever raise from up front, even with a strong hand such as 3-2-A-A double-suited. Two reasons: this is a strong hand and you want to create deception, and you don't want to run off any potential customers.

741. Conversely, if you are holding this starting hand in late position, you will almost always want to put in a raise or a reraise, especially if it is a multiway pot. Most of the players already in the pot will come along for the ride no matter the strength of their hand.

742. If you flop the nuts, bet or raise to try to discourage the long shots but don't go nuts with your nuts until after you see the river card. Then and only then should you raise until the moon turns purple.

Omaha High-Low Tips for the Advanced Player

743. In hold'em you often will raise to try to narrow the field. In Omaha high-low that strategy isn't going to work. When you raise preflop, you will do so to build a bigger pot, not to limit the field. Many good Omaha players will do a lot of preflop raising and after-flop folding, but when they do hit their hands, they will rake in a pot so big a small dog couldn't jump over it.

744. If you are in the cutoff seat or on the button and everyone seems to be entering the pot, there are probably a lot of low cards out making low cards on the flop improbable. If you are holding big cards, raise and build the pot in the hopes that you will scoop and keep that small dog running around in circles. (Metaphorically speaking, of course. Please don't put your poochie on the poker table!)

745. As mentioned, an ace in your hand is preferable. With a wraparound hand such as K-Q-J-10, it is okay to limp into a multiway pot if you are in late position. If you catch good on the flop, preferably with a straight or a straight draw and no low cards, good. If not, muck.

746. Such high-only hands have value when it is multiway and you can get in for only one bet. This situation means that you will receive a good price on your investment.

747. Because playing an ace (or double-aces) is so important, if you are playing in a game with knowledgeable players they know this too. Therefore, if few enter the pot, you can consider that the deck contains some aces (should you need one to make your hand). On the flip side, if it is a multiway pot, the deck is more than likely void of aces.

748. Play your players. Example: If the blinds are solid players and you are on the button and had planned to limp into the pot, but no other players have entered the hand, raise rather than call. Why give the blinds a free flop when, if they bet as solid players, you know you are beat? Raise and hope to take it before the flop.

749. Know your players. Example: If a very tight player raises, he proba-bly has double ace suited with a deuce. So if you're in late position with a 5-4-3-A unsuited that you planned to play, let it go and wait for the next inviting opportunity.

750. Be very careful about defending your blinds in Omaha eight. Remember, starting with the worst hand from the worst position is a lot to overcome, so try to have the best of it if you defend your blind. Be less defensive if a lot of players have entered the pot.

751. Consider your pot odds when you are on a drawing hand. If you are drawing to a nut flush and there is a low hand possibility, check to see how many people are in the pot. When drawing to the nut flush, if you make the hand, you will end up with the winning hand approximately one in three times. So if there is a small pot, wait for the next time before investing too much money. When you win your one out of three, you want to win a huge pot.

752. Many Omaha eight players will automatically raise the pot from any position with double aces regardless of their other two cards. This is not good play. Actually double aces with middle cards are best folded from early position. However, if you are in late position and are single or double-suited with middle cards, a limp is okay. Examples: A-A-10-8 single-suited or A-A-J-7 double-suited.

753. Mix up your play with double aces. Raise from late position sometimes; at other times, just call with them. When your hand does hit, it will probably be the nuts and if you haven't raised, first of all your hand will have a surprise effect and secondly there will be more players in the pot, making a bigger pot for you to win. When you miss, which will be more often than not, you can easily get away from the hand and you got to see the flop for a minimal investment.

754. Know when to speed up; know when to slow down. Example: If you flop the nut flush draw and the nut low, get as much money into the pot as possible. If your opportunity turns into only the low half (or quarter), slow down, just check and call. If you then hit your nut flush card and there is action before you, full speed ahead!

755. There are times to lay down a nut low draw on the flop. Example: You hold A-K-Q-3, single-suited. The flop brings 9-8-2 rainbow. Without runner-runner perfect (when the perfect cards to fit your hand come twice in a row—in other words a very long shot!) you are drawing to win only half and maybe one quarter of the pot. With three overcards, see the turn if you can do so inexpensively. If you get no help, fold and wait for the next opportunity. Being able to fold in this type of situation versus being unable to do so makes the difference in the overall winners and the overall losers.

756. Follow your gut instincts. After the flop, if it isn't just right for your hand, remember the above-mentioned adage, "If you study long, you study wrong." Or, put another way, "If you're in doubt, dump it."

757. By listening to your gut you will, more often than not, save bets. Saved bets in any poker game are as good as money earned; they go into the profit margin.

758. Another way to save bets is to play in such a way that you will get a free card now and then. Example: You are in late position and flop a good draw. If it is bet before you; raise it. The message you are giving is that you have flopped a very good hand. You very possibly will get a free card (meaning no one will bet) on the turn.

759. Slow-playing is often a way to make more money in hold'em. In Omaha eight, slow-playing is never a good idea for a multitude of reasons. One reason is that the majority of hands can be drawn out on. Another is that players will tend to call you down anyway (so go ahead and bet your big hands). Even when you are looking at quads, go ahead and bet. Make any low draws or full houses pay to play with you. If you do end up having to split the pot, there's more to share.

760. Although bluffing is an intricate part of all poker games, especially late in tournament play, bluffing in Omaha high-low, low-limit ring games is fruitless. George Elias states, "Bluffing in Omaha high-low is as smart as facing a rushing rhino!" In higher limits this tip may not apply, but bluffing in low-limit Omaha high-low eight-or-better is definitely risky business.

8.

Five-Card Draw Jacks-or-Better, Jacks-Back, and Lowball Draw

In the late 1880s in California, long before the large, elegant card casinos became prominent in Los Angeles County and before Native American casinos sprinkled the Golden State, all forms of gambling were outlawed, except poker. California lawmakers found gambling to be unacceptable but made an exception for certain games of poker. This legal loophole resulted in a multi-million-dollar poker industry in Gardena, California, which began in the late 1930s.

Gardena became home to six luxurious, success-ful card casinos from the 1960s and remained so for over twenty years. In the 1980s the Gardena monop-oly on card gaming in LA County crumbled when legislation passed to allow other Southern Califor-nia cities the right to open and operate public card clubs. Still, only the games of five-card draw (jacks-or-better to open), jacks-back, and lowball were allowed. There were no house dealers prior to 1981; players rotated the deal (just like at home). It was not until 1987 that a variety of popular games of poker such as seven-card stud and hold'em were legalized in Southern California.

Five-card draw jacks-or-better (to open) and jacks-back begin the game with an ante. Example: If you are playing $5-$10, the ante would be 50¢. In a $10-$20 game, each player would ante $1. Lowball does not have antes; the action begins with blinds. Example: In a $15-$30 game of lowball, the big blind would be $15, and the small blind would be $10. A small limit game such as $2 and $4 would have $1 and $2 blinds. Five-card draw and jacks-back are both played with a joker, but the joker really isn't considered a wild card—it's part of the strategy. I guess you could call it partially wild. The joker can be used only as aces or to complete straights and flushes. For example, it cannot be used to make a full house if you are holding two pair, but if you are holding an 8-9-10-joker and your fifth card is a banana, you could draw one card and if it is a 7 or a jack, then the joker can be used as the jack or queen to complete the straight.

There are only three parts to the games of draw poker, jacks-back, and lowball. They are the deal, the draw, and the showdown. Each game has only two betting rounds. Each player receives five cards facedown, and then there is a round of betting. The betting begins with the player to the left of the button in lowball (just as in flop games); the player who opened the betting will act first after the draw in draw poker. With just two rounds of betting, there's a decided lack of action in these two games so you seldom find them in casinos these days. But they are fun home games for something different.

The object in lowball is to make the lowest hand and the object in draw poker is to make the best high hand. In all three games, the player has three options for his action: he can pass, he can open the betting, or he can raise if someone else has opened the betting. Example: If you are playing 25¢ ante, $1 and $2 limit draw poker, or jacks-back, the opening bettor can bet $1 before the draw and $2 after the draw. The remaining active players who called the bet (or raised) can then discard one, two, three, four, or all five of their cards and draw new cards. The second and last round of betting follows the draw. Most often five-card draw requires a qualifier of a pair of jacks-or-better to open. If this is the case and there are "no openers," everyone antes again. If, on the second deal, no one can qualify, everyone antes a third time. The antes stops after a third time if no one has drawn jacks-or-better to qualify to open the betting.

You can play five-card draw with no qualifier; this is considered to be "guts to open." This game of draw poker with no qualifier is widely known as California draw.

Jacks-back always requires an opening qualifier of jacks-or-better on the first deal. If no one can open, there is no re-ante or re-deal and the game then reverts to lowball.

If you end up loving the five-card poker games, maybe you enjoy living in the past (or maybe you lived in the past)! Five-card games were the most popular in the Old West.

Tips on Playing Five-Card Draw, Jacks-or Better, and Jacks-Back

761. In draw poker, after anteing and receiving five cards down, the action starts to the left of the dealer; if a player has a pair of jacks-or-better he can open the betting.

762. If no one has jacks-or-better, everyone antes again and you have another deal. This can happen a third time with a third ante, but then the antes stop but you continue to deal until someone has openers. After the pot is opened, the betting begins with the opener and goes clockwise before and after the draw.

763. In home games if you prefer, the dealer can ante for everyone. Example: The ante is 25¢ and there are eight players. The dealer can ante $2 for the table. This eliminates the "who didn't ante" problem but in order to be fair, you should agree to play six, seven, or eight games (how ever many games it would take for the antes to come out even among your players). With this understanding, everyone will have an equal amount invested in antes.

764. If this is the case and no one has qualifiers, the deal passes and the next dealer adds $2 to the pot for antes until someone can open or until there are three rounds of antes in the pot. This would be rare, but the deal would stay on the third dealer.

765. You can check on the first round of betting even if you have openers of jacks-or-better. You may want to do this if you have a huge hand, in order to check-raise and win more money.

766. If you check your openers, you are taking a risk. If no one else has openers, then everyone will re-ante and re-deal and there goes your big hand right into the muck. You would check your openers if you had a strong "tell" that someone else was going to open.

767. Jacks or queens can be vulnerable hands. If you do not improve you can lose to two little pair or better. If you are holding a hand like K-Q-J-J-10 in a multiway pot, you may want to unload one jack and draw to the straight, which would be a powerful hand if you make it. This is called splitting openers. If you do this, you must keep one of the cards facedown and close to you to prove you had openers at the end of the hand.

768. It is not bad to have aces for openers even if you are against two baby pair. Aces can become aces-up while the two baby pair must improve to a full house in order to beat aces-up.

769. The odds of improving your hand if you have to draw five cards are terrible, and four-card draws are almost as bad. Don't do it! (Unless you hate your money and your goal is to get rid of it.)

770. If you open and no one calls, you are obligated to show your openers. In other words you cannot bluff that you have openers.

771. If you are against one opponent, you may decide to stand pat on a weak hand, representing a big hand. If he draws and misses and then you bet, he should fold. Watch his body language.

772. If someone has openers and you have an open-ended straight draw, dump it if it appears that you and the player with the openers will be the only two in the pot. You know your opponent has, at the very least, a high pair and you have eight outs to make your straight plus the outs to make a pair, but will your pair be better than the openers?

773. The time to draw to a four-flush or a four-straight is in a multiway pot. If there are, or you believe there will be, four or more players in the hand, you then will have the pot odds for this type of draw.

774. If someone opens and you have two small pair, do not raise. This is a vulnerable hand unless you fill up on the draw. Or, you can stand pat (take no cards) and represent a made hand. This is draw poker semibluffing, as your two pair may end up being the best hand anyway.

775. Draw poker can be played with or without a joker. If it is played without a joker, usually anybody can open with any hand. (Guts to open.)

776. A hand with the joker is sometimes worth a raise or a reraise depending on what cards you have to go with it. Remember, the joker is good as an ace or to complete straights or flushes. Often, catching the joker is opportunity knocking. However, if you have a hand such as 9-7-4-2 rainbow and the joker, dump it. What are you trying to make?

777. If a player has a "pat hand" (they do not want any cards on the draw) proceed with caution. Even if you have trips, a pat hand could easily mean a straight, a flush, or a full house already made. It also can mean a stone cold bluff.

778. On the subject of bluffing, if a player stands pat, knowing how your opponents play and being aware of any body language that will give you a tell to the strength (or lack thereof) of their hand will help you determine if he actually has a monster hand made or just wants you to believe he does. (See chapter 9, "Tells".) To reiterate, knowing your opponents is almost as important as the cards you hold.

779. Remember, bluffing is an intricate strategy in any game of poker. In this game you must have jacks or better to open the betting. A good time to bluff would be if a shy, tight player opens the pot and there are several rounds of antes to be won. Raise him on a bluff or a semi-bluff.

780. Do not raise the opener with two-pair unless it is aces-up. The opener must have openers; therefore, he has one big pair (minimum) and could draw the second pair or three-of-a-kind to beat most two pair hands.

781. When playing jacks-back, the tips for playing five-card draw jacks-or-better apply unless no one can make openers. At that point the game reverts to lowball. (See the following tips on lowball.)

782. If you have a wheel or a baby straight in jacks-back, you have a monster hand in either five-card draw or lowball so you should check and try to induce action to build the pot. Whether you end up playing for the high or the low, you have an excellent hand to stand pat on, and you have deceived your opponents regarding the strength of your hand.

Tips on Playing Lowball

783. As previously discussed, razz and seven-card stud are dealt identically (seven cards and five rounds of betting); the difference is in seven-card stud you are playing for the best high hand and in razz you are going for the low. Five-card draw and lowball work the same way as far as making the best high hand and the best low hand, but you have only five cards to work with and two rounds of betting, which makes the games very different.

784. Do not play five-card draw or lowball with more than eight players. The probability is that you will run out of cards, but if you must and you do run out of cards, shuffle the discards and deal them for the draw.

785. Lowball played with the joker is considered by many to be "California style" lowball because that is the way it was played on the West Coast for many decades. If you are dealt the one and only joker, you are leading the race—if you have small cards—which is not to say you cannot be beaten. If you are dealt the joker with a handful of paints, muck it.

786. Pairs of course are a handicap. If you end up with a pair after the draw and your opponent also pairs, the lowest pair will win the pot.

787. Aces are considered the lowest pair. In the case of a tie, which would be unusual (but not impossible) for lowball, the lowest five cards would win. Example 8-3-2-A-A would lose to 7-6-5-A-A.

788. The best hand in lowball is the wheel or bicycle (5-4-3-2-A). Second best is 6-4-3-2-A, then 6-5-3-2-A, and so forth. Remember you rank the hands from the top down, just as you do in razz. Example: You have 7-5-4-3-2, while your opponent has 7-6-5-3-A. The low A-3 does not win. The winner is your 7-5, which beats the 7-6.

789. It does not take hands this low to win at lowball. Often a player will draw one card to a 4-3-2-A and end up with a king while his opponent takes two cards to his 7-2-A and ends up drawing a 4 and a jack. The jack would win.

790. Straights and flushes do not count as high, but pairs do. You could have a baby straight flush and win the pot.

791. After the draw, the second and last round of betting takes place. The action begins with the player under the gun (to the left of the button).

792. Check-and-raise normally is not allowed in lowball. If you want to allow check-and-raise in your home game, have it understood up front.

793. Because there are only two betting rounds in lowball some will want to play with a kill pot to add action. All players must agree if a game is to be a kill game.

794. Any player can "kill the pot" by announcing, "I kill the pot," and double the normal bet. This must be done after he looks at his second card but before he looks at his third. (Kill games are for those who like to gamble.) Another example of a kill game: You are playing $2-$4 lowball with a $1 and $2 blind. If one player wins two pots in a row, he then has to post a $4 blind (if he is a blind he must add $4 to the blind) and the game goes to $4-$8 limit.

795. If the kill player wins a third hand in a row the kill feature remains in effect. If not, the game reverts to $2-$4 until another player wins two pots in a row.

796. Position is as important in lowball as in any other poker game. Your position should help you determine whether you stay, draw, or fold.

797. In draw games you have no exposed cards to help you decide whether or not you should continue after the deal. Your position and your cards, plus any tells or body language from your opponents, are all you have to work with.

798. You can start with a beautiful low draw and catch a brick. Also, if there are a lot of players in the pot that means there are a lot of low cards out and your chances of catching a baby are lowered.

799. Having the joker in your hand allows you to enter the pot with a poorer hand than you normally would. However, having the joker doesn't always mean you have a winner. It's certainly an advantage to pick up the joker but the best low hand wins, with or without the joker.

800. The fact that a player stands pat does not necessarily mean he has a 6 or 7 low. The following are approximate odds of being dealt a pat hand: a pat 6 or better = 1 out of 290 deals; a pat 7 or better = 1 out of 95 hands; a pat 8 or better = 1 out of 35 deals.

801. To quote the poker scholar George "Profit" Elias, "All pat hands are not created equal." Example: Two players have a pat 8. One has 8-7-6-4-3, called a rough 8, and the other player has 8-4-3-2-A, or a smooth 8 because it is the best 8 possible.

802. Your turn: Which is the smooth 9 and which is a rough 9? Hand #1 is 9-4-3-2-A or hand #2 which is 9-5-4-3-2? It's a close call, but hand #1 is the smooth 9.

803. In lowball you need a good hand or a good draw to enter the pot from early position. You can raise from late position with a weak hand if no one has entered the pot.

804. Standing pat on an 8 or 9 is usually the thing to do if the pot has not been raised. In other words, don't discard an 8 to draw to a 7 or a 9 to draw to a 7 or an 8.

805. If you have a rough 9 on the deal and the pot is bet and raised before it gets to you, let it go. Wait for the next hand.

806. A pat 9 is often playable from middle position as is a pat 10 from late position. Lower hands can be raised or even reraised from late position.

807. Some rules to live by if you want to be a winning lowball player: Never call a raise if you need to draw more than one card. Do not defend your blind. Another Elias tip, "Learn to think of your blind as a rental payment for your seat."

808. Slow-playing is not profitable in lowball. If you have a good (little) hand, bet or raise the heck out of it.

809. If you enter the pot from early position, be prepared to call a raise. If you cannot take the heat of a raise, do not enter the pot.

810. If you have a wheel or a pat 6 on the deal, don't be aggressive from early position. You definitely have the winning hand with a wheel and you probably have the winner with any 6. You don't want to run off any paying customers. Maximize your big (little) hands. But if someone raises, reraise!

811. Bluffing before the draw is seldom correct unless you're playing from late position and no one has entered the pot.

812. Some bluffing don'ts: Beware of trying to bluff a short stack. Also beware of trying to bluff into a herd of players who have checked to you. Beware of bluffing too often; you will get the reputation of being the bully. In order for bluffing to be effective, it needs to be done sparingly.

813. If you believe a player is bluffing too much, pick a time to raise him with a rough hand, maybe even a baby pair. Let the bully know that he can't continually get away with it.

9.
Tells

According to popular belief, the poker term "tell" is short for a telltale sign. While a poker "tell" would come under the heading of psychology in the advanced study of poker, some tells can be so blatant that an observant amateur can pick up on them and put them in his poker arsenal.

Simply put, a poker tell is involuntary or purposeful body language that gives information about you to your opponent on the strength or weakness of your hand. This is the same type of information you can get from your opponent to help you evaluate his hand—a mannerism, a breathing pattern, an eye twitch, a finger movement, a toe tap, an ear pull, or as in the movie, *Rounders,* licking the filling from an Oreo cookie when you have weak holdings! Advanced poker players will set up a tell when they are bluffing and then use it in reverse to confuse their opponents when they have the nuts.

Back in the days when I smoked, a confidant called my attention to a tell I had. When I made a big bet and lit a cigarette, it meant that I had a big hand. I lit up in celebration, so to speak. When I didn't touch my package of cigarettes or my lighter, I didn't have the goods. That was my only tell that anyone ever told me about. I quit smoking (thankfully) and put an end to that particular tell.

If you believe you have picked up a tell on an opponent, watch his play closely. When you are certain you have this tell and know what it means, use it to your advantage. Let's say the player to your immediate left holds his cards slightly off the table until the action is on him when he is going to fold. If he is going to play, he leaves them laying flat on the table. If he is on your left, he has the button when you are on the cut-off seat. If you know he is going to fold, consider the button yours and play your hand accordingly.

Some players refuse to try playing poker on the Internet because they insist that poker is mostly about tells—living, breathing, looking into an opponent's eyeballs tells. They claim they cannot play the game properly if they cannot see the breathing patterns, the faces, the eyes, the hands, and so forth, of their opponents. I say hogwash to that theory. There is so much to the game of poker that tells alone should not make or break a player. There is an exception to every rule and perhaps there are some top notch players who are huge consistent winners because of their talent to use tells to their advantage—never mind the cards, the position, or the luck. If you are one of those rare players, I apologize for the washing of the hogs if I offended you and your best poker talent. According to John Vorhaus, there are even tells on the Internet—so there!

I do not deny that tells are a part of poker. I have picked up on tells before; however, it is not a huge part of my game I get very busy thinking about everything else that is going on in a poker game. If a tell is obvious, I use it, and I do my best not to give off any tells of my own.

I hope the following tips will help you with understanding tells, using them to your advantage, and making even more money.

As you study the tells below, ask yourself if you are guilty of having any of them. If yes, stop!

814. Poker tells from others can be voluntary and used against you as a tool of deception or they can be totally involuntary. People whose hands shake when they handle their chips or cards when they have a huge hand are giving an involuntary tell. Someone who performs an act to try to convince you that he has either a strong hand or a weak hand is giving a voluntary tell. You must study your opponents in order to read their individual tells.

815. I believe the easiest tells to recognize are hand tells. If a player puts his hands on his chips, he probably is going to bet, call, or raise. Some inexperienced players will even count out their chips for a bet, call, or raise before it's their turn. That tells you all you need to know in order to decide how to play your hand.

816. Another obvious hand tell is the "muck position." If the player holds his cards off the table, ready to release, you certainly know his intentions. I have seen pros do this. They are ready to get on with the next hand. This is a terrible habit, but don't tell them.

817. Here's how to use such a tell to your advantage: If you are in late position with a medium-strength hand like an ace-jack and if you know by the hand tells that the players who will act after you are going to fold, you can raise the pot. However, if a player yet to act is a rock and has a hand tell that he is going to enter the pot, you may decide to only call or even fold.

818. If you have a monster hand, you could hold your cards in a muck position only to raise the pot when the action is on you. That is called a reverse tell. You can't get away with it often (especially in the same poker session or if you play with the same people regularly) but an occasional reverse muck-tell will add more value to your big hands.

819. Beware if a player has a pattern to his play and that pattern changes. Often when a player bets aggressively and announces in a clear, loud, and meaningful voice, "I raise," he has a weak hand and is bluffing or semi-bluffing. On the other hand, be leery of the player who tries to sneak quietly into the pot without being noticed. He probably has a monster hand.

820. If a player habitually looks away from the action when he is uninterested, and then he folds, you can assume he isn't a very good player because he isn't paying attention to the game. Beware of the player who doesn't do this usually but then suddenly he does. This will usually mean he has a big hand and wants to appear to be disinterested in hopes that many will enter the pot.

821. The flipside of that tell coin belongs to the player who looks directly into your eyes, especially if he is trying to look mean or intimidating. It's as if his eyes are saying, "Go ahead, call me if you don't like money; I dare you." His heart is probably saying, "Please don't call, please don't call." Staring you down is usually a sign of weakness.

822. Another involuntary tell is the breathing pattern. If your opponent starts breathing rapidly after looking at his hole cards, he has probably just looked at a very good starting hand. However, if he has limped into the pot and starts the rapid breathing after seeing the flop, he probably just made his hand. Proceed with caution.

823. When a player sighs or gives a little negative moan when entering a pot, again, it could be a big-hand tell. Another big-hand tell is if he says in a meek voice, "OK, I'll call."

824. Listen to your opponents. If an inexperienced player labors over calling an unraised pot and says under his breath, "Well, I'll see the flop," that is most likely exactly what he means; he will call and take a look at the flop. If the flop helped his hand or made his hand, he will act accordingly. If he is acting before you and checks, the flop didn't help him. If you are heads up or one other player has checked to you, you should bet no matter what.

825. Likewise, in seven-card stud, if a player says, "I'll see one more card," that is his intention. If he helped his hand, he will stick around; if not, he will fold. Do not check and give him a free card.

826. If you are in a hold'em game and the flop brings three to a flush and your opponent looks back at his cards, he probably did not make the hand. He is looking to see if he has one card of the suit that flopped and how big it is.

827. If a player glances at his chips after receiving his first two (or four) cards in hold'em or Omaha, or his first three cards in a seven-card game, he probably is going to enter the pot. Play your hand accordingly. If he does this after the flop or after fourth street, he probably has helped his hand.

828. A shaking hand from a normally calm hand at a crucial time is usually a sign of a monstrous hand. The experts explain that this involuntary action is a release of tension because this person knows he is going to win the pot. The flip side: if a player raises or reraises with an almost rigid hand he probably is bluffing, especially if he is holding his breath or is breathing unnaturally slowly and steadily.

829. Discovering a tell on an opponent is a wonderful event and you should be proud. Just as important for you is to avoid giving any tells. As for the possibility of your having any tells, put some thought into it. Have a friend watch you play and see if he notices any. Make it a point not to have any.

830. With practice you can control your breathing, your emotions, and your mannerisms. Try playing each hand like a programmed robot, doing the same movements repeatedly, whether betting, raising, reraising, or simply folding. Between hands, come off the robot routine. You're there to have fun in addition to making money. If you cannot control the shakes, use it to your advantage and bluff with it now and then. Pick up a hand in late position, any hand will do, fake shake, and raise that pot! Keep them confused if you have an involuntary tell.

831. If a player lifts his sunglasses to get a better look at his cards or the flop, he probably has a big hand and wants to be sure of what he is seeing. Like, "Wow, I can't believe I flopped a set." Then he will go back to being coy behind his sunglasses.

Introducing Mike Caro

In 1984, Mike Caro, a tremendous poker scholar and teacher, had his book *Caro's Book of Tells* published. Believe me, yesteryear's tells are still alive, well, and on the mark in today's poker world. His poker seminars are profound, he is unconventional, but his teaching is distinct and clear. I learned the following tells direct from the genius. I'm constantly amazed at just how factual his studies are.

832. Players often stack chips in a manner directly indicative of their style of play. Neatly stacked and organized chips mean a conservative player; sloppy means a sloppy player. Chips haphazardly stacked usually mean a careless player.

833. In the absence of indications to the contrary, call any bettor whose hand covers his mouth. This is not 100 percent foolproof, but often a player will put his hand to his mouth (as in real life) if he isn't telling the whole truth.

834. Generally, a genuine smile means a genuine hand and a forced smile is a bluff. The friendlier a bettor is, the more apt he is to be bluffing.

835. If a player acts weak, he probably has a strong hand. If he acts strong, his hand is most likely weak. Don't fall for it and you will save money.

836. Two other signs of weakness: Players staring at their chips are usually holding a weak hand; players reaching for their chips out of turn are usually weak.

837. If a player bets and then looks back at his hand as you reach for your chips, he is probably bluffing. A forceful or exaggerated bet usually means weakness and a gentle bet usually means strength.

838. If a player looks and then checks instantly, it's unlikely that he improved his hand. If a player looks and then bets instantly, it's unlikely that he is bluffing.

839. Players staring at you are usually less of a threat than players staring away. Beware of sights and sounds of sorrow.

840. Last, but certainly not the end from the mad genius: players are either acting or they aren't. If they are acting, decide what they want you to do and then disappoint them.

10.

Home Games

I was born, raised, and educated in Nashville, Tennessee. As an adult, I lived in Atlanta, Georgia, for fifteen years prior to my move to Las Vegas to pursue a career in playing poker and writing about it. Of those years my fondest memories are Christmas, family reunions, and home poker games. As a child I had to sneak to play poker along with my male cousins. We lived in the Bible Belt. Our parents believed poker was gambling, gambling was sinful, and if you sinned you would go to hell! We would have weekend poker marathons in the garage. Our parents thought we were playing monopoly, a reasonable assumption since we played poker on a monopoly board using monopoly money as a camouflage.

I was all grown up and married when I moved to Atlanta where my husband and I played in a poker club twice a month. How I looked forward to those games! Our poker nights were a wonderful social outlet. Poker was something I was good at, a pastime my husband and I could enjoy together and an activity I loved to do and could make money doing. We played dealer's choice (the deal rotates around the table clockwise and the dealer gets to choose the game). I was never fond of goofy games—spit in the ocean, baseball, crisscross, or zigzag. I wanted to play real poker games like seven-card stud, five-card draw, and Texas hold'em. I couldn't win consistently with the silly games or the wild card games. There was too much luck involved.

It seemed I had a natural ability when it came to the ins and the outs of "real" poker. I loved the competition. I loved knowing what some friends were holding because I knew exactly how they played, and I loved seeing my poker stash grow month after month. Still, even all grown up, I didn't want my folks to know about my sinful ways.

In 1975 I was thrilled to find out that a private club in our area held regular poker games. I was devastated to discover that no women were allowed. I eventually brought my stash (which I found out was called a bankroll) to Las Vegas only to learn how little I knew about playing "real" poker. For a year I had a ball playing, and my spouse pressed $50 a week into my palm for my poker entertainment money. It was only after I lost my husband that I was forced to face reality—I had some choices to make when it came to my poker playing. I either had to learn how to win (I knew it could be done because I had watched others win consistently) or at the very least I had to learn how to stop losing. When I faced that realization, I began a serious study of the games.

In my Atlanta days I had never heard of poker tournaments or no-limit hold'em. After my move to Vegas, I discovered poker tournament competition and appreciated the idea of the tremendous overlay. I could take $15 into a weekly tournament and occasionally, when I got lucky, come home with $500 or more. It didn't take many weekly wins to stay ahead.

At this time, the mid-eighties, there weren't many major tournaments around, and of the few that existed, the buy-in was often out of reach. To overcome this, I started a home poker club, and we would play satellites for seats in some of these events. Our winner played as a partner for all of us and if that person finished in the money, 50 percent went to the winner and 50 percent went to the rest of the club members to be divided equally. The first time I won our home competition and got to play in a "real" poker tournament, I won $8,000 for us! I was thrilled—and I have been hooked on poker tournaments ever since.

Here are some tips for running a good home poker club. Have a ball!

Tips on Home Games

841. First, you need to organize a poker club—couples, singles, or mixed. In this day and age, finding eight or nine friends who love to play poker should not be difficult.

842. Second, if you don't have clay poker chips, good cards, and a felt table cover, get online and go shopping. No old-time plastic chips, please. If you ultimately decide to hold one-table tournaments or satellites you also will need a good timer clock. You can find them at any electronics store.

843. In establishing a poker club, you can move your gatherings from home to home, or elect one player who may have the best environment (like a game room with a real poker table) to host the poker gathering. If that is the case, a different club member should supply the drinks and snacks each time you meet. It isn't fair to put this responsibility on one individual or on one couple.

844. If you are so inclined, give your poker club a name, and nicknames are always fun. Prior to your first game, have a poker discussion and talk about what games you want to play and what games you don't want to play. Everyone should have a general understanding of how to play your chosen games.

845. Host a poker seminar prior to your first poker party. Have everyone buy *1,000 Best Poker Strategies and Secrets* for their reference book.

846. In home games you can play any poker game; however I recommend only "real" poker games. This book tells you how to play a variety of games. One game that does not have its own chapter is HORSE. This is a combination of the games hold'em, Omaha, razz, stud (seven-card stud high), and eight-or-better Omaha. They are played in the order listed.

847. Another popular multiple game is HOSE, which combines hold'em, Omaha, stud, and eight-or-better (stud). Although you seldom find HORSE and HOSE in casinos, you can request them at the major tournaments, and they usually are played at high limits. It is fun to play a variety of games if everyone agrees to play all four or five of them.

848. Someone will need to act as the banker before your game starts. The banker will sell chips for money. Be prepared with change for $100 or silver change if you are going to play nickel, dime, quarter. At the end of the evening, the banker will then buy the chips back.

849. If you want to take your poker club one step further, you can offer satellites for major tournaments. Elect a president and the most important officer of your club, the treasurer.

850. Take a vote on which tournament you would like to send a representative to. Next, figure the buy-in you will need to achieve this goal. Be sure to include reasonable travel expenses.

851. If you live in Memphis, Tennessee, for example, go online and check the major poker tournament schedule in nearby Tunica, Mississippi, rather than someplace far off like Las Vegas. You might pick Jack Binion's annual World Poker Open, the $10,000 championship event.

852. If you're all rich, you can have a single one-table satellite with ten players and charge your players $1,000 each. The winner will not need travel expense money since Memphis is just a hop, skip, and a jump from Tunica.

853. If you're not rolling in dough, break it up into weekly or monthly satellites. This is where your treasurer will be so important.

854. Let's say yours is a monthly club with ten members. Each month, each member will pay $100 towards the tournament buy-in. (You can begin these evenings with the continuing contest and end them with real money games, or play the real money games as part of the contest.) You will keep a big score board. Using a point system, one point will be awarded to the first player eliminated, two points to the second, on up to ten points for the winner. You accumulate your points and at the end of ten months, the player with the most points wins the $10,000 seat.

855. If you want to play for the $10,000 buy-in for the WSOP in Las Vegas but don't live nearby, figure in an amount for transportation and accommodations for the winner. With that in mind, your buy-in could be $110 per game, or if you play every other week it would be $55.

856. I am familiar with a poker club in Kokomo, Indiana, called the "Top Ten Club." They have a logo, jackets, shirts, and hats—the works. They play weekly and accumulate enough money during the course of a year to send their biggest winning player to Las Vegas for a week to play in the big event of the WSOP and have every member of the club come along as the cheering gallery.

857. Another good idea is to have your winner play for 50 percent of the prize pool of your chosen major tournament with the other 50 percent being divided among the remaining players. That way, if your club has a winner, everyone wins!

858. The division of any win should be up for discussion. Your players may prefer 60-40 or 70-30; they may even vote for winner-take-all but it sure is fun to have partners. At many major tournaments I will see a player on a cell reporting to the poker club back home how he/she is doing. Great, positive, long-distance energy.

859. You may prefer to send several players to a major tournament to play some of the preliminary events with buy-ins ranging from $500 to $5,000. Be creative. This could ultimately be a moneymaking proposition for your club.

860. When playing satellite poker at home, the only problem is that when one or two players are eliminated, their evening of poker is over. Have two poker tables set up for just this instance. Eliminated players can play together outside the confines of your tournament.

861. When the first player is eliminated, have him be the dealer. After three or more are out, start your second game for real money. You might win your buy-in back!

862. If you have a passel of poker-playing friends and are energetic, enthusiastic, and motivated, start a poker league. For a poker project of this magnitude, you will need several leaders.

863. Mirror a bowling league. Local businesses can sponsor a team of poker players. The cream will rise to the top to play in a playoff with other league winners. It can stop there or go further, sending the top players to a major tournament. Imagine the excitement if the front page of your hometown newspaper screamed, "Nuts McGraw of the Squirrel Creek Hardware Store Poker Team Wins the World Series of Poker!"

864. Here are some other poker club ideas. Have a potluck dinner and poker night. Hire one or two baby-sitters (paid for out of poker money, of course) and have all the kids stay together in one home. That way the kids also get to have a special night of fun.

865. If there are teenagers available (in addition to the baby-sitters) and interested, teach them to deal (they may already know how as so many young people are playing poker these days). All players should put a set amount of money ($3 to $5 each or more depending on how many hours the kids work and how many players belong to your club) into the dealer/baby-sitter fund. Like baby-sitting, a teen can make some spending money with his "part-time gig."

866. If you send a member of your club to a major event and he does well, be sure to let me know…it will look good on my résumé! Good luck!

867. The following is a good no-limit hold'em structure for a poker satellite or tournament. If you use this structure and have twenty-minute rounds, your satellite should last a total of approximately four hours.

868. The faster a tournament or satellite goes the more the luck factor comes into play. The longer it lasts, the more important the skill factor. If you need to shorten the time period, cut the rounds to fifteen minutes and eliminate a few of the rounds. Add your potty breaks at will; usually every third round is often enough. Stop the clock and take five.

869. Start each player with $1,000 in chips. (You can start with more but it will lengthen the time of your competition.)

Satellite Tournament Structure

Round	Ante	Small Blind	Big Blind
1	$25	$50	$0
2	$50	$100	$0
3	$75	$150	$0
4	$100	$200	$0
5	$100	$200	$25
6	$200	$400	$25
7	$300	$600	$50
8	$400	$800	$75
9	$600	$1,200	$100
10	$1K	$2K	$200
11	$2K	$4K	$400
12	$3K	$6K	$600
13	$4K	$8K	$800
14	$6K	$12K	$1K

11.

Internet Poker

The first Internet poker (IP) emporium opened in 1999, experienced great success, and the concept has grown beyond belief in popularity. As the poker phenomenon spread across the world, so did IP. Anyone with the desire, a computer (or access to one), and a love for the game can be playing in cyberspace within minutes. They can play for free, for pennies, dollars, or millions of dollars via satellite tournaments. If Internet poker had been around in 1985, I might still be living in Atlanta, Georgia, rather than Las Vegas where I visited regularly and eventually moved to in order to play poker. Internet poker is the absolute nuts for anyone interested in learning poker, playing poker, practicing poker, teaching poker, or for those who love the challenge of playing poker but do not live in an area where they can easily get to their local casino or public cardroom to participate. That's the good news. The bad news is that many things people enjoy safely in reasonable quantities can become addictive, and Internet poker is now on that danger list. In all fairness, folks with addictive personalities can get addicted to all sorts of things—activities, exercise, food, drink, drugs, even religion. Any addiction can wreak havoc on families and relationships, so it's important to keep IP playing to a safe and fun level.

For more information or for help with problem gambling, you can contact the National Council on Problem Gambling (confidential 24-hour hotline: 800-522-4700) or Gamblers Anonymous (213-386-8789; www.gamblersanonymous.org).

There are, of course, plenty of good things about Internet poker. You don't have to shower and get fixed up to go out in public; you can play in your pajamas or naked if you so desire, unless you live in a glass house. You don't have to drive, park, walk, or tip. If you're a smoker, you can smoke! If you're not a smoker, you don't have to put up with the smell or the secondhand smoke.

The games are much faster than casino games and you can play more than one game at a time if you desire. You can parlay a little bitty bit of money in online play to humongous land-based poker tournaments where you can win mega-millions if you are one of the lucky ones!

I know a man who was rendered a quadriplegic due to an accident in 1997. He was a strong, energetic, motivated, active young man before the accident. Understandably, he became withdrawn and depressed after. He told me he had wanted to kill himself but found it impossible without the use of at least one limb or even one hand and with no one who would agree to assist him. In 1999, his church took up a collection and bought him a computer. He learned to operate it by using a point stick held between his teeth. This was the beginning of a new life for him. He now has a voice-operated computer. He can write, correspond with friends, and travel the world via cyberspace. Anything he is interested in, he can research and learn more about. He discovered a new passion when he found poker on the Internet. One of the activities he most missed after his accident was his weekly poker game with his buddies, even though his friends brought the game to him now and then. He now has access to poker anytime he takes a notion to play and no one has to hold his cards or handle his chips for him. I'm sure there are many stories about Internet poker being a God-sent activity for shut-ins.

Unfortunately, there is a possibility of collusion between two players or a whole herd of players online, but this doesn't bother me much at all. I know too many people who are good poker players who win fair and square regularly and I personally know folks who are involved on the "inside" of

Internet poker and they have explained to me the systems that are in place to monitor players. If they believe there is any collusion going on, or any monkey business at all, they take immediate steps to put a stop to it. The Internet poker rooms are making way too much money to allow any bad press or negative gossip. They want their sites to be as clean as a whistle with immaculate reputations so players will want to keep playing there.

Now back to the good stuff! There is a tremendous selection of games and limits to choose from online. If you can't find what you're looking for at one site, you can jump to another with the click of a mouse. And with the anonymity of playing online, your opponents won't know who the donkey is when you make a bonehead play, so you can't embarrass yourself.

Respected poker genius and elder statesman of poker Doyle Brunson, author of *Doyle Brunson's Super System* and *Doyle Brunson's Super System 2* has said, "What took me decades to learn, these kids can get on the Internet. What I learned by brute force, dealing out hands, they learn on computers. It tends to make for fairly technical players, but they make up for it with aggression, the kind that comes when you learn things fast."

Fast indeed, consider this: an online site can generate ten thousand hands a week. By contrast a pro playing in a casino gets in about thirty thousand hands a year. In a game where experience is so important, this speed teaches new players quickly what the old pros had to work for years to learn.

As you can see, I am a big fan of Internet poker and I believe the good far outweighs the bad. With that in mind, do yourself a favor. If you have not yet discovered playing real poker online in the comfort of your own home, don't waste another minute. First read this chapter, which will make your first visit much easier. We won't go into much game strategy as we have already covered that in preceding chapters. How to play winning poker online is the same as how to play winning poker in brick-and-mortar poker rooms or in your home games. Playing winning poker is playing winning poker wherever you choose to play.

If after reading this chapter you would like more great online poker information, pick up a copy of *Killer Poker Online* by John Vorhaus and *Internet Texas Hold'em* by Matthew Hilger, both of which I highly recommend. You'll LOL (laugh out loud) while reading Vorhaus and learn all there is to know about the mechanics of online poker as well as gobs of great strategy. Hilger will instruct you on how to win at Texas hold'em online (or you can choose to use his theories in brick-and-mortar rooms).

Welcome to the wonderful world of Internet poker.

Tips for Playing Poker on the Internet

870. Before deciding to play poker on the Internet, take a good long, look at yourself. If you have an anger management problem or are highly emotional, don't play. Computers are expensive and if you throw one out the window or take a sledgehammer to it after a series of bad beats, Internet poker may not be for you. I actually know a young man who buys mice (or is that mouses?) by the dozen. His frustration comes out in the form of slamming his mouse down so hard that he breaks it. He also has thrown a few of them against the wall so hard that they dent the wall and fall to the floor in pieces (like it was the poor little mouse's fault). He fusses and cusses, fumes and spews—and then goes right back for more. Of course, he does one hell of a happy dance when he wins. I'm not sure which he does the most, abuses his mouse or dances.

871. One more warning: if you get hooked on Internet play, the day will come when, at a key moment, in a key hand, your computer will crash and burn. It may be something simple or something major, but the timing will suck and you will get upset. If you can handle the infrequent hazards of cyberspace poker then please proceed. (Get good and you could have a standby laptop, paid for with winnings, at the ready for just such a wretched mess.)

872. A computer glitch is one of the biggest differences in Internet and live poker. The only way such an unforeseen incident could happen in a B&M room is if you dropped dead at the table. If this happened, I assure you that some smart-ass player would ask if your hand were also considered dead, especially if you had a death grip on the winning hand.

873. Visit several (or dozens) of the Internet poker sites before starting to play. They come in all sizes: super-size, large, medium, and small. Once you are on the site, click around, look at the games, and check out the options. Just like with other sites, the more you click, the more you will learn.

874. All of the rooms will have hold'em and no-limit hold'em. If you are looking specifically for Omaha, seven-card stud, stud high-low, or other games, you'll need to visit some of the larger rooms. The largest sites are partypoker.com, ultimatebet.com, and pokerstars.com. For medium and small Internet poker rooms, jump on a search engine and see what you find. There are passels of them, and you may find your comfort level there.

875. I often will visit one of the smaller rooms if I want to play a tournament with one hundred or fewer players. There are Internet poker tournaments with one thousand, even two thousand-plus players. I played in one with five thousand players, which was the maximum number of players they could accommodate. The reason for the multitude of players was the price…it was free!

876. There is a wide array of options available to you at most IP sites— from sound effects (some dealers actually speak while some sites will beep when it is your turn), backgrounds, the chat feature, (yes, you can chat with your fellow players), avatars (a character you may choose on some sites to represent you on screen), to the color of the deck of cards. If you have a question and you can't find the answer, go to "contact us," email them, and they will respond. Do this with a variety of sites and then decide where you will first play Internet poker and get ready for a treat.

877. Once you choose a site where you want to play, download the software. To best play poker on the Internet, you will need Windows 95 or above, 100-MHz Pentium or faster CPU with at least 32 MB of RAM, screen resolution of at least 800 by 600 pixels with 256 colors, and 6 MB of free disk space. A PC is much better for poker play than a Mac and this is stated with no offense meant to Apple products. It's just a fact of life. (Thank you, John Vorhaus, for this information.)

878. If you don't understand the last tip (frankly, neither do I except the PC versus Mac part), just pick a site that looks interesting and follow the directions for downloading. Believe me, if I can do it, you can do it!

879. Having a cable or a satellite modem is the best set up. The higher the speed the better; however, you can use dial-up. I have known many players who started out playing poker online with their dial-up connection. It works, but you have to be patient when making the initial connection. Once these individuals got hooked on playing online they switched to the highest speed cable they could find, paid for with winnings!

880. Make the decision about which room your premier online poker experience will take place in and then register there, and choose an online identity and password. The site will ask for some information through a minimal sign-in procedure, which will allow you to participate with play money. This is a great teaching and learning tool.

881. I strongly suggest that once you decide that you want to play poker online you keep a file or an index card in your safe or in a safe place with information on each site where you play. Keep your screen name and password for that location on each site's card or file. You probably won't stay on just one site and your screen name and passwords will in all likelihood change. I am registered on a dozen sites and if I don't visit one for weeks or even months at a time, I'll often go back only to go blank on who I am at that particular site.

882. When you choose a screen name, many of the names like TheNuts, Champ, Kissmyace, RiverRat, and so forth will be taken. Come up with your own. You may or may not want to be gender specific: MsWildCard or MilwaukeeStud. You may or may not want to be age specific like, Soccermom, CollegePkrGenius, PrettyGirl23 or aces4Grandpa. I know a gruff seventy-eight-year-old male pro player whose screen name is Daffodil. Once you have registered you are ready to play.

883. Begin in the free games. I don't care if you are an advanced poker player and the best player in your hometown. You need to begin in the free games to get the feel for how to play poker in cyberspace. The speed with which the hands are dealt will be a surprise to you. Learn what to click to call, raise, reraise, fold, or be dealt out while you go potty, put the laundry in the dryer, or grab a quick snack.

884. The free game is also the place to test out all the options you will have to chose from. You may find you prefer a purple table top to red or the blue deck to the green. Try all the options just to see what is available. You may want to chat or chatting might annoy you, so you will want to know how to turn it off.

885. Once you're finally ready to play for real money, you need to open an account. Go to the cashier and again follow the instructions. At this point you will be asked for more pertinent information. There are a number of ways to fund an account. This process can take from minutes to a week or more, depending on how you choose to go about it. You can use a credit card. You can also send a bank draft, a cashier's check, or a money order to the site, but these methods all take time. If you choose one of these methods, that's fine. You can continue to play, practice, and learn in the "Monopoly money" games while you wait for your real money to be received.

886. There is a service offered on the Internet that is sort of a cyberspace bank. It's an online holding house for your money, which allows you to have cash at hand for when and where you might need it in an instant, sort of an online ATM. If you shop online, you may have already discovered Firepay or NETeller, the funding routes that I recommend. Again, the cashier will direct you on how to open this type of account.

887. It will take a few days to get these options set up, but it will be worth the wait over the long run. Once they are set up, depositing or withdrawing money is quick as a snap.

888. Be sure to look for deposit bonus promotions before depositing any money. There is almost always a promotion for a new player or any player who needs to "reload" his account. No need to miss out on free money or free stuff.

889. Even though you have had practice in the "play money" games, be careful and pay attention now that you're ready to join the game for real money. Watch where your arrow is located and remember how easy it is to click...the wrong button.

890. True story: I have a friend who was playing in one of the bigger online tournaments. She had played a flawless game for four hours and was delighted to be on the final table with a healthy chip stack. Her cat ran across her laptop, which clicked on the "Call" button (this could have been avoided if she had the arrow away from any of the action buttons). She called an all-in bet with a 3-9 offsuit and lost all her money. She won money for her seventh place finish, but she was on her way to a much greater win. The chat went wild, players and observers couldn't imagine what had gotten into her. She meekly typed, "The cat did it." (Personally, I might have been scrapping cat guts off the wall. I'm joking, cat lovers! But if it happened with my beloved poochie, losing thousands, maybe even tens of thousands, would have given me puppy-throwing thoughts.) The moral to this sad story: pay attention and watch that action arrow!

891. Begin your real money play in the low limits and remember, just as in brick-and-mortar poker rooms, play only with money you could afford to flush. As you gain experience and build your bankroll, you can move up in limits.

892. Mathew Hilger, a professional Internet poker player and author of *Internet Texas Hold'em,* suggests the following recommended bankrolls if you plan to play a lot (this scale is based on playing one hundred hours or more). For $.50-$1 limit games, a $500 bankroll; for $1-$2 games, an $800 bankroll; for $2-$4 games, a $1,200 bankroll; for $3-$6 games, a $1,800 bankroll; for $5-$10 games, a $2,500 bankroll; for $10-$20 games, a $5,000 bankroll; for $15-$30 games, a $7,500 bankroll; and for $20-$40 games, a $10,000 bankroll. The ideal scenario is to begin play at the low limits (there are games that can be played for pennies if you desire) and move on up as your bankroll grows from your poker prowess.

893. Remember, just as in B&M poker establishments, you can change tables. If you are not comfortable in your game or the limit you are playing, bow out with a click, go to the lobby, and find another game. Likewise, if you don't see a game that tickles your fancy, go to another site.

894. One of the beautiful things about playing poker online is the ability to "hit and run" (play one or two hands and leave). It can be done in B&M, but it's a bit embarrassing to sit down, win two big pots, then get up and leave—and in home games, forget about it! After word of your hit and run tactics spread, you could be blacklisted from any future invitations anywhere in your hometown or state!

895. Another beauty is your multitasking ability. You can play poker while you check your email, pay your bills, watch *Casablanca,* or talk on the phone. If you're lucky enough to have wireless, the options are almost limitless—cooking, eating, having a manicure, having a pedicure, clipping your nose hair, your ear hair. Need to go potty? Take your laptop with you! Nobody has to know…

896. However, while you're multitasking, make sure you pay attention to your game. Act when it is your turn. Don't make your tablemates wait for you over and over again. Though it actually is only seconds, it can drag on if you are a repeat offender and those seconds seem like minutes.

897. Multi-tasking can help you to be patient while waiting on the proper starting hands. Almost everything you have learned about playing winning poker can and should be used in Internet play, including hand selection. Patience remains a virtue in any poker game anywhere.

898. Another positive aspect of playing on the Internet is that you can always find a game to your liking no matter what time of the day or night. Like the old saying goes, "It must be the cocktail hour somewhere in the world." Likewise, folks from all parts of the world are playing twenty-four hours a day, seven days a week, and on holidays.

899. You also can play multiple games. I personally believe that if you really want to play poker properly, one game at a time is plenty but two isn't totally unreasonable. I may play two games if, while I am running really well in a ring game, a tournament I signed up for has started. I know hyper kids (of legal age, of course) and adults who seem to be "action addicts" who play three or more games at one time. Some sites have a minimize button to make the table small so you can have four tables on your screen at one time. I think this is ridiculous and can't imagine how anyone could win doing such a thing.

900. If you do play multiple tables, do not add multi-tasking on top of that. You need to be totally focused on your games so you don't leave your tablemates continually waiting. That is rude and unfair. You will see chat postings that read, "zzz," meaning, "We're going to sleep because you're making us wait so long, you donkey!"

901. Keep this in mind: if you are not a winning player, don't even consider playing more than one table at a time. Why lose two or three times faster? The idea is to win more in a limit within your comfort zone.

902. With so many hands being dealt per hour, your good starting hands will come more often—and so will the bad beats. It will seem as if you see more aces getting crushed online simply because you're seeing so many more hands being dealt.

903. Your position is just as important in your strategy on the Internet as in a brick-and-mortar environment. Hands you will fold up front, you can play from late position, and if no one has entered the pot you can raise with them.

904. Winning strategy is very much the same on the Internet as in B&M; the only difference is the speed and the lack of tells in IP. You simply cannot see the breathing patterns or nervousness of your opponents and other such hints about the strength of their hands. However, as you get more advanced in Internet play, you will want to read what John Vorhaus writes at length about cyberspace poker tells in his book.

905. Keeping records of your play is easy; you know how much you deposited and you know what your balance is. In a click, you know how much you are winning or losing.

906. If you play a lot you should keep more detailed records. I keep records of ring games and tournaments, what limit I play, whether it was a satellite, a one-table or a multi-table tournament, what game I was playing, and where I was playing. Study your records to discover your strengths and weaknesses. Then adjust your play to what is most profitable for you.

907. As in casino games, I recommend you do not show your hands unless you have to. Why give out information?

908. If anything happens online that upsets you (besides bad beats), contact your customer support and they will look into it. Legitimate complaints include foul language, a screen name that you find offensive, or your suspicion that there is some collusion going on. Jot down the day, the time, your game number, the name of the offensive player, and the table number. This is the information that will expedite a solution to your problem. I know from experience that complaints are taken care of.

909. One difference in Internet play and B&M is that you don't need to vary your play so much. Your opponents also are multitasking or playing multiple tables and not paying great attention to your style. Also, sessions are often shorter than in casinos or cardrooms.

910. The exception to this is in a big tournament online. When you are in the running for a potentially big win or to win an expensive prize package to a big land-based tournament with all expenses paid, stop any activities that will take your mind off the task at hand and totally concentrate on the game and your opponents.

911. Online tournaments are a hoot and can be such an adrenaline rush. They can give you the opportunity to play levels you could never play in a ring game ($2,000 and $4,000 and higher!) and the best part is the overlay. In the "old days" of live tournaments, if I couldn't make ten times my investment with a win, I didn't think it was a good overlay. Today, you can make a hundred times your investment and sometimes more!

912. You can find online tournaments for as little as a dollar for practice up to $100, $200, $300, and $500 and all price ranges in between. The higher prices may sound unafford-able but you can play $10, $20, and $30 satellites to win a seat in the more expensive competitions. You can even play a $2 or $3 tournament to win a seat in the $20 or $30 tournaments in which you can win a seat to play in the $200 or $300 tournaments where you can win a great gob of cash, or you might win a $10,000 entry into a mega-tournament in a casino where you can win millions! I'm telling you, it has happened before, and it will happen again.

913. Never forget the "regular guys" who paid less than $100 online, won a prize package worth $11,000 that included a trip to Las Vegas, accommodations, expense money, and a buy-in to the main event of the World Series of Poker in 2003 and 2004. Chris Moneymaker and Greg "Fossilman" Raymer made poker history and became millionaires and Internet folk heroes, all for a very small initial investment.

914. When you do decide to play a tournament online, be sure you have enough time. Big multi-table events with a thousand plus players can last four or five hours or longer.

915. Is bluffing possible online? The answer is yes and no. I would not attempt bluffing in low stake games, $3-$6 and less, especially in limit games. The players simply will call to "keep you honest." On the other hand, in one-table sit-n-goes (a one-table tournament that usually pays the top three players out of ten) as the limits go up you may have to bluff a hand or semi-bluff to survive. Again, the higher the cost of the event, the better a bluff will work. Don't even think about it early in the competition. In the early rounds you should be playing as slow as molasses in the winter. It's later, when it's time to start moving and shaking, that you will consider a well-timed bluff. Never try to bluff a player who has already entered the pot, and never try to bluff more than one or two players at one time.

916. An example: (I will admit, I never thought about this one; it's another Hilger Internet tip) You will find yourself in small blind versus big blind situations a lot more on the Internet than you would in a live game since in a live game you often "chop" the blinds) bluffing with trash hands in these situations can often be profitable. If neither player raised preflop, you have to win just once every three hands for your bluffs to break even; therefore betting out the flop from either the small blind or the big blind can often be successful.

917. The bottom line is this: solid, straightforward good play will ultimately win the money for you. To be successful over the long haul you also need discipline, patience, and good money management skills.

918. Most Internet players are social players. There is no reason your online poker hobby cannot be profitable, but you must practice and use what you have learned about playing winning poker. You may find that you can supplement your income while enjoying poker in cyberspace. This is a reasonable and achievable goal.

919. Last, and quite possibly the best part of IP, is the cashing out process. First, win a chunk of money and then cash some out and do something special. Again, for your first cash out, just follow the directions. They will send you a check (that's the long way) but if you took my advice and opened a FirePay or a NETeller account, they make an immediate transaction from the Internet account to your cyberspace bank and in a few business days it'll be in your bank account waiting for you.

Now go forth to your computer, play poker, have fun, and make money.

12.

Brick-and-Mortar Card Casinos and Poker Rooms

Millions of people all over the world love to play poker at home with friends and family, on the Internet, or both. In all probabilities they eventually will have the opportunity to play in a "real" poker arena. If they live in an area near a casino, their opportunity is practically in their own backyard. Although it is an experience they desire, nine times out of ten the thoughts of first entering a poker casino or cardroom will cause some anxiety and intimidation. It reminds me of when I was a kid on summer vacation from school. Once a week one of the moms would take a bunch of us kids to one of the local swimming pools. There were two huge public pools in our neck of the woods and several smaller ones. When "pool day" arrived it didn't matter whether we were headed to the big facilities or the smaller ones, we always were so excited and happy at the thought of spending the day enjoying the water. I vividly remember the first few times I got to go. Everyone was so delighted and excited at the thought of our day of fun in the sun as we gathered our necessities—picnic lunches, suntan lotion, goggles, beach towels, floats, and pool toys. I didn't know about the rest of the kids, but although I was excited and looking forward to the experience, I also was scared to death. I knew in my heart it was going to be a day of great fun but that first plunge haunted me. Would I sink? Would I freeze from the cold water? Would my bathing suit come off, leaving me buck-naked and embarrassed to death? The other kids never knew of my fears, and once I eased into the water, my apprehension quickly faded and I had a blast.

It isn't easy for most to take that first plunge into live poker, but once your body crosses the card-room threshold and you get used to the environment, you'll have a wonderful time because you will be prepared. By the time you leave, you will look forward to your next visit.

920. Like the public swimming pools in the days of my youthful excursions, poker establishments come in all sizes. They all have one thing in common: management and owners want you to have a good experience so you will return.

921. When you enter a poker room or poker casino initially, the first person you should encounter will be an employee who will greet you and make you feel welcome. This might be a floorperson, a dealer on "front of the room" duty, or in the case of some of the huge poker casinos in Southern California, the concierge. Advise this person that you are a new player because his job is to make you feel comfortable and show you the ropes.

922. Your greeter will answer any and all of your questions. If you are visiting a small room, the employee can give you a short tour or simply point out the different games, and explain what limits are being played at what tables. If you are in one of the larger poker casinos, the greeter or concierge will answer your questions then direct you to the area of the casino where the games and limits you are interested in are being played. There, another floorperson will take over and find you a seat or put you on the list for a seat and show you where you can wait.

923. When you are seated, if the dealer has not been advised that you are a new player, then you should tell him. He should watch you, guide you, and be very patient while you tip your toe in the poker pool for the first time and then ease on in for a good time. Poker is known as a social game of great camaraderie in addition to a fun means to make a little money and maybe even to supplement your income.

924. Even though I loved to play poker at home, it took me three visits to Las Vegas before I finally worked up the nerve to sit down at a poker table . I finally consumed some liquid courage and took the plunge. When the very friendly brush (person who greets you at the front of the poker room) took me to my seat, he asked me if seat three was okay. Because he led me to my seat, I didn't have to worry about which way to count around the table to know where seat three was. The seats are numbered, beginning with seat one to the dealer's left, in a clockwise formation. See the chart on page 2 for a visual.

925. The tables are also numbered. A floorperson may tell you table eleven, seat seven. However, if he knows this is your first visit, 99 percent of the time he will take you under his wing and guide you to the correct table and seat.

926. The Bicycle Casino in Bell Gardens, California, even has a poker college you can attend. In addition to teaching whatever game you are interested in, part of the "course" is to introduce you to the nuances of playing public poker. Integrated in the poker school course is a complete tour of the facility including a look behind the scenes. (The kitchens are huge!)

927. Before beginning play, you will have to buy chips. Normally, there will be a chip runner whose job it is to take your bills and bring you chips. Often the chip runner will have a wide belt-type apparatus on his waist with chips in huge pockets. He is like a human cash register. It is nice to tip this person a buck, but not an absolute.

928. Normally, casinos or card clubs do not want you to play with cash or to have cash on the table. There are exceptions of course. Some poker establishments will allow you to keep extra money under your chips but it must be in plain view. (Beware of the player who asks, "Can I buy more chips?" in the middle of a hand of poker!)

929. Poker is a service business. I advise tipping everyone. If you plan to allow yourself $200 for your first buy-in, make it $210 and have tips for all, including the cashier, when you cash out. As previously mentioned, tip the dealer when you win a decent sized pot. A toke is not expected if you take a tiny pot. I believe generosity will come back to you ten-fold. Good karma.

930. Each game will have a "minimum buy-in." I suggest you buy at least double the amount of the suggested minimum. Example: The buy-in is $40 for a $1-$2 limit game. Buy in for $80 or $100. In bigger games if the minimum buy-in is $100, buy-in for $200 or $250. It gives you a better table image, but do not buy in for more than you can afford to lose—just in case. And do not buy-in for ten times the minimum even if you can afford it. It isn't necessary and it makes you look like you either have gotten into the wrong game or are trying to be a show-off.

931. If your first live poker experience is going to be traveling to a casino to play in a poker tournament, go a few days early to acclimate yourself. Play in a few ring games to get the feel of playing at a "real" poker table. In major tournaments, nobody will take the time to show the new players the ropes; there are just too many of them to try.

932. Go to the tournament area the day before your event and get the feel of the room. Sign up and find your table so you'll know exactly where you need to be when the "cards are in the air."

933. If you win an entry to a major live tournament by playing online, be sure to play a few small buy-in tournaments in a live poker environment prior to your big event. Also be sure that your online poker site has purchased your seat. Do this well before the beginning of your event just in case you need time to get any oversight taken care of. Playing tournaments online is very different from playing tournaments live and in person with other real people, and you need to be prepared for those differences.

934. There is a story of a player who was surprised at the slow speed of the first live tournament he played. Living, breathing human poker dealers simply cannot deal as fast as the dealing online. The player kept getting preoccupied because there was so much time between hands (compared to Internet play). The dealer kept having to tell him when it was his turn. At one point it was his turn and the dealer said, "Sir." No response. The dealer knocked on the table, "Sir, sir, the action is on you." The player was not even looking at the dealer. Finally the dealer mimicked a computer and said, "Beep! Beep!" The player then acted and the other players at the table broke up.

935. Don't play when you are tired or hungry. Most poker rooms serve drinks and many serve liquor but you should play smart; don't drink alcohol when you are playing serious poker.

936. If you're partying, it is a social evening, or you do not care if you win or lose because you're just there to have a good time, that's another story. If this is how you play serious poker, however, you will be ensuring that the other players at your table are having a good time because they will be winning your money.

937. Many poker rooms serve food. Some charge (usually very reasonable prices), and they will roll a little side-table right up to you. You can order a snack or a full steak dinner.

938. If you decide to eat at the poker table, it is okay to sit out for a few hands. Just tell the dealer and he will not deal you in until you advise him that you are ready. (This is not true during tournament play—you will be dealt in no matter what.) If you decide to continue to play while you eat, pay attention and don't slow up the game while you butter your roll. Do not get crumbs or grease on the cards.

939. Many casinos will offer food comps. "Comp" is short for complimentary. The way to know if you can get a comp is to ask. Some rooms may require a certain number of hours of play in order to offer a comp. If this is the case, ask to be tracked or request a player's card.

940. If you have not been playing long enough for a comp but you want to grab a quick bite, ask about a line pass. This will allow you to go to the front of the buffet or restaurant line.

941. On TV you often see players wait until the action is on them to look at their cards. The reason, or so it goes, is so no one can pick up a tell on them when they peek at their holdings. I disagree! In waiting until the action is on you, you are losing some thinking time. Granted some hands are no-brainers (you know you're going to fold) but if you look at your cards immediately as you receive them, you can then start looking around the board for needed cards or watch as other players look at their cards. It also speeds up the game.

942. Don't be an actor or actress. If you're going to fold, fold! If you're going to play, make your bet, call, raise, or reraise. If you need time to contemplate, that's okay, but it is not necessary every hand.

943. The exception to the rule: it is okay to "go Hollywood" if you have a monster hand and are figuring how to get the most money in the pot you are going to win. You can "act" as if you are going to fold and then change your mind and so forth. I have seen some performances that deserve an Academy Award. Don't fall for it. See the chapter on tells for more on this subject.

944. If you play a hand to the river, always turn your cards faceup for the dealer to read. There will be occasions where you are going after one hand and make another without realizing it. Example: Let's say you went after a four flush but didn't make it. The hand is checked on the river. Betting ends, and it is time for the showdown. Some players will just muck their cards because they missed their draw. But don't you do it! Turn your cards faceup; you may have a winner with a baby pair or an ace or even a king high. Until you have had twenty years of experience playing live poker, always let the dealer read your hand. Over the long haul, this will make money for you.

945. When you do have the winning hand, hold onto your cards until the pot is awarded to you. Mistakes can be made and if your cards happen to end up in the muck, you will not receive the pot. You don't need to have a death grip on your cards, just a finger or two on them to protect them is fine.

946. When you decide to play a hand, listen to what the other players are saying. You may hear some valuable information. Example: In a game of seven-card stud if a player says, "I'm going to take one more card," he probably means it. If he doesn't help his hand and he checks, you should bet no matter what because if he had decided to take "one more card" and got no help; he likely will fold. If he took one more card, and helped, he'll be sticking around.

947. In a split game, Omaha high-low in particular, never assume you will be splitting the same pot. Example: If you have an ace-deuce for low and also made a pair of 4s, don't assume that your opponent also has an ace-deuce because he has a bunch of low cards and that he also made a high hand. He may have an ace-3 and no pair for high and think he has the best low when, in fact, you're going to scoop this pot!

948. If you have the nut high in a split game, raise 'til the cows come home or you run out of money, whichever comes first. You don't want to do a bunch of raising with the nut low (for reasons explained in the Omaha high-low split chapter), *but* when you're heads-up and have the nut low against what you believe to be another nut low, keep raising.

949. Another example: You are heads up in Omaha high-low and you're holding A-K-Q-2. The flop comes J-7-3 rainbow, the turn is a 5 and the river is a 10. You have the nut low. It is certainly possible that your opponent is going high and you will split the pot but what if he has only an ace and a 3 and he is going low? Do not assume! He could have misread his hand and believe he made a high. You could have a scooper and you just checked because of your assumption that you will be splitting the pot. Remember the fitting cliché: to assume is to make an "ass out of u and me."

950. Once you are comfortable in your new poker environment and have begun to converse with your tablemates, never ever ridicule another player's play. If he is playing badly, why on earth would you want to embarrass him and risk losing him? He is a fish. We love fish! Even if you hate all seafood, you gotta love the fish!

951. If you are at a table and you can't identify the fish after fifteen or twenty minutes of play, be careful, you may be it! Time to change tables. Look for greener pastures (or cooler waters). If for any reason you are not comfortable, ask for a table change.

952. There is a famous player nicknamed "Tuna." He acquired the name when he first began playing poker in a small public cardroom in northern Nevada because he was the biggest fish they had ever seen. Some fish study their game and become sharks; Tuna is one of them.

953. If you are not comfortable because you are crowded and squished between two other players at one end of the table, while the players at the other end of the table seem to have plenty of elbow room, ask the dealer to "square the table." This means in a ten-handed game, players four and five should be sitting directly in front of the right and left point of the dealer's tray. If it is a nine-handed table, player five should be directly in front of the dealer. Don't take it upon yourself to get the players in their proper spots. That is part of the dealer's job. Just quietly ask the dealer to square the table. He will know exactly what you mean.

954. If you find yourself in a game with a player who is continually putting in a straddle, doing anything that upsets you, or just plain getting on your last nerve, change tables. You do not go out to play poker to be aggravated. Quietly ask the floorperson for a table change.

955. All cardrooms in America request that only English be spoken at the poker table. This is to prevent any collusion in a foreign language.

956. Speaking of foreign languages, if you are visiting a European country where you will be playing your first public poker game, check out the situation before appearing at the poker club. Some clubs in Europe are private, but all you have to do is join the club prior to showing up. Some require a certain dress code that isn't as casual as is allowed in America.

957. You often will see a player show his cards when he doesn't have to. It is usually with either a big hand or a bluff. My advice is to never show a hand unless you have to. Anytime you show a hand you are giving information. The less information your opponents have on your play, the better.

958. Always play in turn. It is your turn when the player to your right has acted. If you act before it is your turn, it isn't the end of the world, but if your action is a raise because you have a big hand, you might lose a player who would have been in the pot if you had waited until it was your turn.

959. You may not be familiar with the term "chopping the blinds" that can come up in ring games but not in tournaments or online. This means that if all players fold and only the blinds remain, they can agree to "chop." When agreed, players will take back their blind money. Some players will almost always agree to chop while others never chop. If you agree to a chop, you need to chop every time during your session. To chop one time but discover you have a big playable hand at another and raise is considered unethical. If you chop, you chop, and if you don't, you don't.

960. When you are in the big blind of an unraised pot, do not fold because you have a crappy hand. You get to see a free flop, and it just might be a crappy flop that matches your crappy hand. I have won some huge pots just because my big blind wasn't raised.

961. This is a case in point of raising if you're going to enter the pot from late position. You don't want those blinds catching a flop.

962. When you want to raise a pot, say, "I raise." Don't whisper or mumble; be audible. In no-limit, this allows you to call the bet and raise whatever amount you want to in order to get the job done; in limit games it gives you the time (and lets others know your intentions) to raise the proper amount.

963. String betting is not allowed. If you put money out and go back to your stack for more, you've made a string bet. This is why it is so important to announce your raise. Do not give a thumbs-up sign for your raise. Say it, unless you cannot speak and then hand motions are acceptable.

964. Do not "splash the pot." This means don't throw chips directly into the pot. Put your call, bet, raise, or reraise in front of you. Each player's chips will be in front of him until the action of the particular round of betting is complete and then the dealer will pull the bets into the pot.

965. Do not expose yourself at the poker table. If you expose your cards before the action is complete, your hand is considered dead whether you showed your hand accidentally or intentionally.

966. Most serious players begin a poker session playing their absolute best. After thirty minutes or an hour of waiting patiently for a playable hand, they begin to revert to old habits of playing too many hands and ultimately losing. Play your A-game each and every time you play. If you find yourself playing anything other than your best, it's time to call it a day or night and go home.

Class dismissed. Now go play poker and have fun winning money!

13.

Poker
Table Protocol

If you are an invited guest to someone's home for dinner or invited as a guest to a public restaurant, you know what to do and what not to do. You wouldn't eat your soup with a fork, or pick up the bowl and slurp it. You wouldn't rinse your fingers in your water glass or pick at your toes or your nose. You know what is proper and what is not. You know what is polite and what is rude, what is acceptable or unacceptable.

Whereas slurping soup in America is frowned on, in Japan it's not only okay, it's considered complimentary to slurp one's noodles and broth.

Lithuanian dining customs are unique and rigid. The head of the household sits in the place of honor at the end of the table along the wall. The other men sit along the wall with the women sitting across from them. Another Lithuanian dining custom involves the slicing of the bread. It is something of a ritual. It is considered a sacred duty done only by the head of the household. On the subject of slicing: for anyone to put a knife down with the sharp edge facing up is to invite misfortune.

Did you know that when served hot tea in a restaurant or teahouse in China, it is customary to tap two bent fingers on the table as an expression of thanks? Not to do so is considered rude.

In Brazil you are never to touch any food with your fingers. Using the hands in direct contact with your food is considered ill mannered and unhygienic. Brazilians use utensils for pizza, sandwiches, fruit, and chicken. If food is to be picked up and eaten with the hands, it is carefully wrapped in a napkin. Brazilians wipe their mouths after every sip of liquid taken. They keep both hands above the table while eating. The American habit of keeping one hand on the lap is considered odd. To use the fork to cut anything is considered rude.

In Arabic countries and India you are to eat or pass food only with your right hand. Even if you're a leftie, you must manage. There is a reason. It is for sanitary purposes. What they do with their left hand leads them to avoid eating with that hand. And that's all I am going to say about that.

In some Middle Eastern and European countries it is considered impolite to eat everything on your plate. Leaving food is a symbol of abundance and serves to compliment the host. To clean your plate is to suggest that you were not served enough food. It is an insult.

Many of you have not had the opportunity to visit any or many of these countries. I hope those of you who have been guests in other countries have taken some etiquette lessons beforehand so as not to embarrass yourself.

My point is that what we do in our country, in our own homes, or as visitors in our friends' homes, may not be the right thing to do elsewhere. We may even make gargantuan mistakes while trying to be polite and do our best, just because we don't know any better. The same is true at the poker table. If you have been a home player for fifty years or if you have played regularly on the Internet for fifty hours a week, when you enter a brick-and-mortar poker room, the rules, the rights, the wrongs, and the manners are different. After reading and committing to memory the following rules of protocol at the poker table, you can make your very first visit to a live poker emporium and feel right at home. You will not accidentally make a donkey out of yourself, or worse, do anything that will inadvertently affect your win rate (or someone else's) at the poker table.

967. Handle your hole cards in such a way that only you can see them. Cup your left hand around your cards and lift the corners with your right thumbnail—unless of course you're left handed, in which case you would do it backwards.

968. It actually is against the rules to "break the rail" with your cards. This means to pick up your cards, take them toward you, and move them over the rail of the poker table. You shouldn't pick up your cards at all. Practice at home; cup your hand around your cards, make a little cave that only you can peek into. It is okay if you have to bend your head down a bit to see your cards. The point is that you and only you see your hole cards.

969. If you feel clumsy and have always picked up your cards to see them clearly, practice more. It is unfair to the majority of the table and to you to expose yourself (your cards, that is) at the poker table. Of course the players to your immediate left and right won't mind; they will have an advantage in the game because they will know what your cards are. It's rather easy to win at poker if you know exactly what your opponent is holding!

970.

On the subject of looking at your hole cards, some poker professors preach to take a quick look at your cards, memorize them, and then do not look back. Your poker teacher (me) says it is okay to look back at your cards as often as is necessary. As you get started in poker, you are going to have a lot to think about so if you need to take a second or third peek, it is okay. I have often seen new players make mistakes because they thought it was a bad habit to take a re-peek at their cards. Why risk thinking you have a nut flush when in fact you have one heart and one diamond? You would be even more embarrassed if you announce a heart flush and turn over the losing hand…all because you were trying to be cool and look superexperienced by not looking at your cards again when the three hearts showed up on the flop.

971.

If you are going to enter a pot, never touch your chips before the action gets to you. This is a tell. It is revealing to the other players at the table about what you are going to do. For example, a player who acts before you plans to raise with a marginal hand, but if he knows that you intend to enter the pot or raise any bet (and he already knows that you are a good solid player), he may decide to just call, or he may even fold because he already knows what you plan to do.

972. If you watch poker on TV you probably have seen Chris "Jesus" Furgerson play. He is a stone face when he is involved in a hand, and he acts exactly the same with every hand whether he is going to call, raise, fold, or reraise. He doesn't move a muscle until the action is on him. He sits with his hands under his chin. He thinks a moment and then acts. No one has any idea what he is going to do.

973. You can create your own style but do it the same every time you are dealt in a hand. I sit with my hands in front of me just over my cards but leaving the cards visible. When it is my turn, I react.

974. This brings up another subject. Don't hide your cards. If you have gorilla hands, be sure you do not completely conceal your cards during the play of a hand. The dealer needs to be able to see them as do your opponents.

975. When you are going to fold, don't throw your cards at the dealer as if you're throwing a softball. Don't get fancy with your mucking. I have seen the twister muck, the under-handed-flip-twist muck, and the ho-hum-sigh-it's-so-hard-to-release muck where the dealer has to reach for the cards. Don't toss your cards on top of the flop. Gently move them toward the center of the table within easy reach of the dealer. A light flick of the cards with your fingertip in the direction of the dealer is fine. Even picking your cards up and deli-cately flipping them with two fingers toward the muck is fine but remember, keep them facedown.

976. If you play correctly you will have plenty of folding practice and you will develop your own style. Just be sure your style does not expose your cards.

977. Do not hold your cards in a "muck" position (making it obvious that you are going to fold) before the action is to you. This is another tell that lets everyone know you are not going to play this hand. Your opponents should have no read on what your action is going to be until it is your turn to act.

978. If you need to leave the table, do not do so until the action is on you. If you are in late position and decide to run to the restroom, do not receive your cards and leave the table when the action is up front. This goes beyond a tell, it is a scream! This bad habit is rude and unfair because it is announcing your action before it is your turn—it can affect another player's play.

979. On the flip side of the mucking coin is the protection of your cards when you are going to play a hand. This is especially important if you are sitting to the right or the left of the dealer. He is like a machine as he runs the game and if you aren't protecting your cards he easily could scoop them into the muck. I have actually seen a player in seat one raise a pot and he had no cards! What's even funnier is, he won the pot!

980. You can simply keep your hand or a couple of fingers on your cards. (Remember to leave a part of your cards exposed so everyone knows you have a hand.) You can also put a chip or two on top of them or use a card capper.

981. Whether folding, betting, raising, or reraising, always act in turn. Your turn is immediately after the player to your right has acted. If you are in seat one and you do not have a clear view of the player to your right because he is in seat ten with the dealer between you, the dealer will look at you when the action is on you. Whichever seat you are in, the dealer will look at you when the action is on you. He sometimes will point to you. He will never embarrass you, but if you are not paying attention, he will do what is necessary to let you know the action is on you. Example: He may pat the table and say, "Sir (or ma'am), it is your turn."

982. If you are in a tournament, always have your big chips visible. Do not stack your $5, $25, and $100 chips in a row and place your $500 and $1,000 chips behind them where they cannot be seen. Every player at the table should easily be able to see your "society" chips, as I call them. This also is true in a ring game. The reason is so that a player cannot eye your chips and believe that he has more than you and make a hefty bet to try to get you to fold, when in fact you have several thousand more than he does. He should be able to see at a glance your approximate chip count.

983. This tip is very important, so please read it over and over until you are sure you get it. In limit games, if the player to your right announces, "Raise," it is okay to go ahead and muck, even if he is fumbling with his chips. However, if you are playing a no-limit game this is not okay. You need to wait until the player who is raising has completely finished his action. The reason is that in no-limit a raise can constitute any amount from twice the amount of the big blind to everything in front of you. If the player to your right says, "Raise," and you immediately fold before he has said how much he raises or before he had completed his action, you could cause a chain reaction. If the raiser knows that three or four people are going to fold to any raise, he can increase his raise amount to insure the remaining one or two players also will fold. Or, if he has a huge hand, he will raise less to try to entice a call.

984. If a player is being verbally abusive or upsetting you in any way, do not argue with him. Between hands, get up from the table, find a floorperson, and quietly explain the problem. It will be taken care of and the offender never has to know who squealed.

985. Please, no cell phone calls at the poker table. Some poker establishments have this as a hard-and-fast rule, but even if they don't, be polite enough to stand up and walk a few feet away from the table to take or make a call. Be even more polite by turning your cell phone off when you are at the poker table.

986. It is okay to converse with your tablemates at the poker table. It is known as a social game; however, don't talk or laugh loudly. Although your partner in conversation is interested in chatting, some players at the table have no interest and it disturbs them. It depends on the makeup of the players in the game. In some cases everyone might listen and laugh at jokes; in some cases only one end of the table may be interested in such and such a football game and so forth. Get a feel for the terrain.

987. If someone makes a bonehead play, don't call his attention to it. You will embarrass him and frankly, why would you want to give poker lessons at the table? If your opponents are making long-shot donkey calls, good for you. They may get lucky and suck out once in awhile but that too is okay. In the long run, bad players will lose.

988. In a brick-and-mortar poker room, do not help the dealer by moving the button, making change, or putting two antes together. Helping the dealer will, more often than not, confuse him and end up taking more time, not less.

989. There are a few exceptions to the "don't help the dealer" rule. When you fold in the game of seven-card stud, turn your upcards facedown and muck all your cards together. Some people just push their cards away from them with the downcards down and the upcards up and the dealer must separate and turn the upcards down. Good stud players fold with all cards facedown automatically. If you are disgusted with the way the hand is developing, be disgusted with your cards facedown as you disgustedly fold. Don't do as some moody players do by just pushing their mishmash of cards away from them as if the cards had cooties.

990. Another "help the dealer" tip is to push your blinds or antes far enough in front of you that the dealer can easily reach them without stretching—or in some cases, short-armed dealers actually have to stand up in order to reach far enough to retrieve your blinds or antes. The dealer pushes the pot to within easy reach for you; show him the same courtesy.

991. If you have to put an oversized chip out for a blind or ante, the dealer will make the change. You are not allowed to do this yourself. There is a story that goes like this: A poker player showed up one day at his regular brick-and-mortar poker emporium. He had a cast from his shoulder to his fingertips. An acquaintance asked what happened to him. "I tried to make my own change from the pot," the wounded man replied.

992. Do not slow roll. To slow roll is to have the best hand and tease the loser by very slowly showing your hand or making a joke. It is not funny; it is rude and unappreciated. Example: The board is 4♥-Q♣-4♦-7♣-10♥. A man holding a pair of 7s has a full house, 7s full of 4s and feels confident that he will win the pot. Another man has made quad 4s on the flop. The full house proudly shows his hand and waits for the pot to be pushed to him. The man with quads takes his time and then says, "I just have two pair. Two pair of 4s!" Not funny—rude! If you took a survey among regular poker players about the things they hate to see at the poker table, slow rolling would probably top the list.

993. Do not tell bad-beat stories. I hate to tell you this, but nobody cares. If any player has played much at all he too has experienced the bad beat you want to tell him about. Let it go. Move on.

994. Don't be a crybaby or throw fits. Phil Hellmuth can't seem to help it; just don't mimic him. It isn't cute or entertaining, and people will simply laugh at you and make jokes about you.

995. It is okay to stand up, talk a walk, or visit another table to chat with a friend between hands. There is a "one player to a hand" rule, so if you try to have a conversation with your buddy while he is in the play of a hand you will be politely reprimanded. It is okay to leave the table to go to the restroom or even to grab a bite to eat if you don't plan to take too long. They simply will hold your seat for a certain amount of time. However, do not leave if you know you are going to be gone for an hour or more, especially if there is a waiting list for the game. Pick your chips up and get back into a game when you return.

996. It isn't a good idea to leave cash on the poker table. If you need to go to the bathroom or leave the table for any reason, leaving your chips is fine, but if you have bills under or beside your chips, pick them up when you leave the table. It would be nice if everyone were honest, but that just isn't the case in the real—or the poker—world.

997. The exception to this rule is if you have just ordered a drink when nature calls. Always tip the waitresses, whether you're physically at the table or not. If you must go before your drink arrives, leave a dollar in your cup holder or lying on the rail of the poker table in front of your seat. This practice is common, and the waitress will know that the dollar is intended for her.

998. If a flop comes with two or even three of a kind and you were holding one of the cards, do not display any dramatics. Example: The flop brings two or three jacks and you folded a jack preflop. Do not say, "Oh, no," or slap the table or your forehead, or groan, or moan. All of these "tells" let the entire table know that you folded a jack. That could destroy the strategy of a player in late position who had decided to represent that he was holding a jack.

999. Do not get angry with the dealer when you have a bad beat. He is just the delivery person. It is not his fault if you are having a bad day. If he could control what cards were dealt to what person, he and his special someone would be very wealthy, and somebody else would be dealing your cards.

1000. Last but not least, almost always tip the dealers. They are paid a minimum wage and their income depends on tokes. I say almost always because if you just win the blinds or antes in a small-limit game, you would be giving them half your profit with a dollar tip. They don't expect that, but when you do take a decent pot, take care of the delivery person.

14.

My Friends Give Big Tips

Since 1986, I have been blessed with a career that I love. That is the year I moved to Las Vegas and found my place in the poker world. That is the year I had my first article published in the one and only poker publication available at that time. Today there is an abundance of poker publications and I am honored to write for many of them.

I was a poker junkie before poker was popular. As I traveled from state to state (Nevada to California back in those days) to play poker and interview poker players, I never dreamed what poker would become. As I wrote poker columns, mostly human interest stories, I had the privilege of meeting many famous or soon-to-be-famous poker players. Some of today's superstars were literally in kindergarten or even diapers when I discovered the unique world of poker. To watch some of these young men and women (some not so young) progress from struggling (even broke on occasion) pro players to tremendous successes in the poker arena constantly gives me goose bumps of pride. Some are multimillionaires today, and some are so popular and busy with their poker careers and requests to make personal appearances and endorse products that they have had to hire entertainment agents or managers. Even with their extremely busy schedules, they made time to chat with me (often through email) about my big project, *1000 Best Poker Strategies and Secrets*.

The following are tips, suggestions, hints, and comments about poker, or quotes from my friends, the famous poker players, most of whom were honing their poker skills long before the "poker renaissance." These wonderful poker pros are generous folks who are willing to share some of their knowledge and wisdom with you, through me.

Doyle Brunson

Doyle Brunson is poker's living legend. From Longworth, Texas, he began his poker career as a true Texas rounder. He has gained great wealth not only with a long string of tournament wins but also by playing the highest-limit cash games in the world. He has won ten World Series of Poker (WSOP) gold bracelets, tying with Johnny Chan for the most won as of 2005. He also has won the world title twice, 1976 and 1977, also tying with Chan. Ironically, he won both world championships holding the same hand, 10-2, and making the same hand, a full house (10s full of deuces), giving the poker hand 10-2 the nickname "the Doyle Brunson." He was inducted into the Poker Hall of Fame in 1988 and into the Poker Walk of Fame in 2004. In 1977, he published the first famous how-to poker instructional book, *Super System*, which rapidly became known as the poker bible, and updated that work in his *Super System 2* in 2004. He is often quoted as saying, "No-limit hold'em is hours of boredom and moments of sheer terror."

Read on for Doyle's tips on final-table play of a major tournament:

"If you are lucky enough to make the final table, you need to evaluate your position. For example, if you have second-place chips and there are several short stacks, you might try to avoid any major confrontations until several players are eliminated. This depends on your financial situation and your desire to win the tournament. If you really need the money and you have a comfortable chip position, you can often assure yourself of a second- or third-place finish by playing carefully. That will result in a very nice payday for you in these ever-increasing large tournaments.

"However, if your main interest is winning the tournament, this is a prime situation to really play aggressively and try to get closer to the leader or even overtake him. The difference [in money] between fifth place and first place is so huge that most players are just trying to hang on so they can be pushed around in most pots.

"My main objective has always been to win the tournament. Even before I was financially secure I always did what I thought was best to achieve my goal of winning first place. You need to think about these things before you start a tournament and decide what is best for you. So if you are lucky enough to get to the last table, you'll be ready."

Todd Brunson

Todd Brunson must have poker in his blood. His famous father, Doyle Brunson, writes in his book *Doyle Brunson's Super System 2,* "'The apple doesn't fall far from the tree' is certainly true when it comes to my son, Todd Brunson. In 1989, after three years of college where he was studying to be a lawyer, Todd stunned me by announcing that he wasn't going back to school for his senior year; rather, he was going to become a professional poker player. I didn't even know he knew how to play poker! So at the age of twenty, Todd started his career as a pro."

It didn't take long for young Brunson to hone his skills. At age twenty-one, he won his first major tournament, the main event in the Diamond Jim

Brady tournament at the Bicycle Casino in Los Angeles. That was the first of ten major career wins, including his first WSOP bracelet in 2005, which he earned by winning the Omaha high-low split event. With that tremendous achievement, Doyle and Todd Brunson became the first ever father and son to capture coveted WSOP gold.

Many saw the heartwarming sight of Doyle Brunson chanting his son's name. When Todd looked at his dad, Doyle removed his trademark Stetson hat and bowed to his son after his victory.

Todd Brunson excels in all games of poker but is a master at high-low split games, so much so that his father asked him to write the detailed chapter of seven-card stud high-low eight-or-better in his *Super System 2* book.

Todd preaches his "Platinum Rule" for any split games:

"The object of split games is winning the whole pot, also known as scooping. This is the most important concept. I can't emphasize this point strongly enough. You've heard of the Golden Rule? Well since this is twice as important, I call it my Platinum Rule. When you are deciding whether or not to enter a pot or proceed to the next street, you should always ask yourself, 'Can I scoop this whole pot? Or am I playing for half?' If you are playing for only half, strongly consider folding. Just like the Continental Divide separates the eastern and the western United States, this concept separates mediocre players from great ones.

"If you have any aspirations of rising to the top in poker, you must learn all the games, especially eight-or-better. These games are almost always included in the mixed games."

Vince Burgio

Vince Burgio is a familiar name and face in the world of poker. He has been a professional poker player for decades, and he also is a regular columnist for *Card Player* magazine. Vince has a wonderful demeanor at the table, always a gentleman and a true sportsman whether he wins or loses. He is known as being one of the gentlemen of the game. One of Vince's proudest poker moments occurred when he won Best All Round Player at the 1992 Four Queens Classic. (At the time, the Queens Tournament was one of the biggest on the tour.) In addition to the title and bragging rights for a year, he also was featured on the cover of *Card Player,* and won an additional $10,222 and a diamond ring. More recently, he won three consecutive tournaments at the World Poker Classic in April of 2005 at the Plaza in Las Vegas and followed that up with two first-place finishes at the Ultimate Poker Challenge in July of 2005, again at the Plaza. This prompted him to adopt the nickname "Plaza Vince."

Vince's list of money finishes in major tournaments is a lengthy one. He has been in the winners' circle of the WSOP ten times over the years and won his first gold bracelet (I'm sure it won't be his last) in 1994 (winning in the seven-card stud high-low split competition), and coming in fourth in the main event that same year.

Here's Burgio's advice on limit hold'em:

"Don't try to get too fancy. If you only play the premium hands it will be enough to win. If you're new to the game don't worry about position and number of players in the pot, just playing those types of hands will almost always be correct. Once you begin to understand why it is correct to play premium hands you can graduate to more hands. Some hands will become playable because you will have three-, four-, or five-way action. Other lesser hands become playable because you have good position. By and large, play your good starting hands with some aggression. Once you master and understand these ideas you should be able to see other opportunities where it will be correct to play lesser hands. These hands may involve more risk but because of the circumstance—number of players, your position, or the weakness of a player—you can make winning plays with lesser hands."

Mike Caro

Mike Caro was called "Crazy Mike" in the early days of his poker career. In 1977, when Doyle Brunson first met Caro, he labeled him the best draw poker player in the world. Since then he has evolved into the world's foremost authority on poker strategy, psychology, and statistics, and his nickname has changed to the "Mad Genius of Poker." He has numerous books, videos, and audiotapes available for those interested in a higher education in the study of poker, in addition to the Mike Caro University of Poker, Gaming, and Life Strategy, which he founded with an online campus.

I first attended a "Mad Genius Mike Caro" seminar in the mid-eighties. As this rather wild-looking man in a green corduroy suit walked back and forth from one end of the stage to the other, arms flailing, he preached specific points of poker, life in general, and lots of psychology directly related to playing winning poker. He kept repeating himself. At first I thought, "No wonder he is called mad." But as I listened, it all became crystal clear. He repeated his most important points to be sure everyone got it. He was smart enough to know that everyone else's mind didn't work as quickly as his did.

The following tips are from the Mike Caro University:

- Money you don't lose...buys just as many things as money you win.
- What you already have invested in the pot...doesn't matter.
- You don't get paid to win pots. You get paid to make the right decisions.
- Tables with laughter are the most profitable.
- In poker...the profit comes from your right.
- Sit to the left of loose players. You want them to act first.
- Beating strong foes wins much respect and little money. Beating weak foes wins little respect and much money.

- Don't bet a medium-strong hand into a frequent bluffer. Checking and calling earns more.
- When a frequent bluffer checks to you...don't bluff.
- You should sandbag powerful hands...when the player to your *left* is the most likely bettor.
- Never criticize weak opponents for bad plays. It makes them uncomfortable and motivates them to play better.
- Never compliment weak opponents for good plays. It makes them proud and motivates them to play better.
- Players staring away...are almost always more dangerous than players staring at you!
- A player who isn't breathing...is probably bluffing.
- Don't watch the flop...watch your opponents watch the flop.

Johnny Chan

Johnny Chan is one of the most recognized individuals in poker today. He won back-to-back world titles in 1987 and 1988. Amazingly, he almost made it a Triple Crown but placed second to Phil Hellmuth in 1989. He holds the record (tied with Doyle Brunson) with ten WSOP gold bracelets in a variety of events. He was inducted into the Poker Hall of Fame in 2002. Chan was immortalized in the movie *Rounders,* playing himself as the greatest poker player in the world.

Chan's tip is on money management:

"In any poker game, money management is the most important thing. You can be a great player and win, win, win, but if you can't manage your money, it's all no good."

Take it from someone who knows.

T. J. Cloutier

T. J. Cloutier has been a professional poker player since 1956 when, as a very young man, he traveled the Texas poker circuit looking for the biggest games. Since then he has won more than fifty major tournaments. Some highlights in his career include winning six (as of this writing) World Series of Poker bracelets. Although the world title has eluded him, he has been "close enough to smell it" on four occasions, placing fifth, third, and second (twice). However, he has won many other $10,000 championship events. He is the only man ever to win the Diamond Jim Brady main event three years in a row—1990, 1991, and 1992. He is the only man ever to win a world title in all three Omaha events—Omaha high, Omaha high-low, and pot-limit Omaha. He played his way into two Tournament Player of the Year awards—in 1998 and 2002. He is coauthor of three popular poker books, *Championship No-Limit and Pot-Limit Hold'em, Championship Omaha,* and *Championship Hold'em.*

T. J.'s advice covers limit and no-limit hold'em:

"In no-limit hold'em the strategy is not where a

lot of people think, which is moving all in all the time. You can maneuver your opponents in no-limit by how you bet the hand. The whole idea is to get as much money as you can out of any given hand that you play. It is very much a game of position. Limit hold'em is so different. It is a game of *big* cards. Play big cards and don't make frivolous calls. Actually, in limit, you need to play tighter than in no-limit. Watch and learn how everybody on your table is playing and play them individually."

Barbara Enright

Barbara Enright started playing cards with her older brother when she was four years old. They played old maid, war, and her favorite, five-card draw. As a young adult, she was a professional hair stylist. Between haircuts, she rushed to the back room to join in on the private poker game that was usually in progress. In 1976, a friend told her about "real" poker that was available in a place called Gardena. Daily, she would get off work and rush to one of the clubs in Gardena. By 1978, after starting at the lowest limits and working her way up as she learned the nuances of the games, she had thoughts of becoming a professional poker player. "I just seemed to have a knack," she explained.

For years Barbara played poker but she also kept her job as a safety net. She soon admitted that she made much more money playing poker full time. She discovered tournament poker in 1986 when a friend suggested she go to Las Vegas and play in the ladies event of the World Series of Poker. "What's the World Series of Poker?" she asked. She soon found out when she went to Las Vegas and made the biggest parlay of her life. She bet $11 on a horse because she liked its name, Victory. She won $75 on that race and played in a $75 satellite to the ladies event of the WSOP. She went on to win that event and $16,400 (from her initial $11 investment). After discovering tournament poker, she set the poker world on its ear, burning up the tournament trail. She is the only woman ever to win three World Series bracelets and the only woman to make it to the final table of the main event, placing fifth in 1995. She also was the first woman to win the best all-round award at the Legends of Poker at the Bicycle Casino in 2000, which paid her a wheelbarrow full of cash and a brand new candy-apple red PT Cruiser. Today, Barbara continues to play poker professionally.

Barbara's tips are on playing position both in limit and no-limit hold'em:

"In limit hold'em, playing position is very important. You can see more flops in limit especially if it's inexpensive. You also can play more hands under the gun or from middle position. You can play hands such as A-J, K-Q, and small pair in addition to stronger hands because you know that someone can't force you out before the flop (normally). In no-limit, position—especially late position—becomes even more important. You can't play such hands up front that you can in limit. You can't call hands on speculation like you can in limit hold'em because they can force you off the hand and then you have wasted money by making early position calls."

Maureen Feduniak

Maureen Feduniak, originally from England, is the grandmother of four and is often respectfully referred to as the Grand Dame of Poker. Her interest in the game developed when she met her soul mate, Bob Feduniak, in New York in 1992. He was a social poker player and she was intrigued when she sat behind him and watched him play.

She and Bob sat on the floor and dealt out poker hands as he explained the nuances of the game. She eventually started playing low-limit and tried her first competition poker in the WSOP ladies event in 1997, where she placed fifth. She states, "At that point I got the bug!" For her higher education, she hired her friend T. J. Cloutier to coach her. She has placed at many major tournament final tables but her proudest moment came when she beat Howard Lederer at the Bellagio's 2003 Festa al Lago $2,500 no-limit event. When heads-up play began, Lederer had her out-chipped five-to-one. This victory would be a tremendous accomplishment for any poker player. Most people recognize Maureen from the 2004 WPT Ladies' Night episode and other major tournament final table appearances.

Maureen is also a champion ballroom dancer.

Her poker tip is:

"I think the principal difference in the strategy of limit and no-limit hold'em is that limit is a game of chase and defense and no-limit is a game of attack. In limit there are more gray areas while no-limit is more black and white!"

Phil Gordon

Phil Gordon was a child prodigy who began college at age fifteen and got his degree at age twenty. At age seven he started playing poker with his great-aunt Lib for pennies. He tells a poignant story of love and respect for his aunt, Marie Elizabeth Lacus, the woman who taught him how to play poker. He lost her to cancer in the fall of 2002.

Phil began donating to the Cancer Research and Prevention Foundation every time he won money in poker competition. He is the man behind the World Series promotion "Put a Bad Beat on Cancer," in which he solicits poker players to pledge 1 percent of their tournament wins to cancer research. In the first year of the event, Chris Moneymaker made his pledge for Gordon and his charity program then went on to win the main event and $2.5 million. The Cancer Research and Prevention Foundation promptly received $25,000 from that single donation. Every year, Gordon has a booth set up for any and all players to make their 1 percent pledge. He is known as one of the nicest guys in the poker world.

Today Phil is known not only as a great poker player, having won millions of dollars during his relatively short poker career and coming within three men of winning the world championship in the 2000 WSOP, but also as an expert poker analyst and the cohost of the popular TV show on Bravo, *The Celebrity Poker Showdown.* He authored a book, *Poker: The Real Deal,* which is dedicated to his Aunt Lib.

He considers his tip simple but important in any poker game or tournament:

"The goal of poker is simple: when you have the best hand, get your opponent to put as much money as possible into the pot. When you have the worst hand, put as little money as possible into the pot."

Barry Greenstein

Barry Greenstein is another generous, charity-minded poker player. He is famous for his poker achievements, and he also has achieved a lot of notoriety for his philanthropy. He donates his poker tournament winnings to charity to help underprivileged children.

Like many in the inner workings of the poker world, I thought Greenstein was a gazillionaire, having made his fortune in the stock market, through an inheritance, or as one story circulated, because he had begun a software company, sold it at a young age, and retired to spend his fortune playing poker. Like those many other misinformed poker players, I discovered through Barry's book *Ace on the River* that none of that is true. He is a hardworking professional poker player who makes a very good living and donates his tournament winnings to needy children because he believes it is a good thing to do and wants to inspire others to consider such generous acts.

He did work at a software company, but he never owned it or sold it. He took the job in 1984. It was close to a poker club in Palo Alto, California, where he spent a great deal of time supplementing his software income playing poker. He moved up in limits through the years, and now he plays the biggest games in the world, along with his friends the Brunsons. Doyle Brunson has stated that Barry Greenstein is in his top-ten list of all-time best poker players in the world.

He is a WSOP bracelet winner and a World Poker Tour Champion. He has many tournament wins under his belt and is known as the modern-day Robin Hood of poker. He is most definitely the most respected man in poker.

In 2004 he published his first book, *Ace on the River*. Even for those who haven't mastered the art of reading, his book is worth the price for the awesome full-color photos on almost every single page.

Greenstein is a shy man, but he relishes the national publicity his charities receive when he wins money in a poker tournament. In his book he explains his decision to donate all of his tournament winnings. He states, "I have felt a need to justify my role in society. I like to think of myself as a modern-day Robin Hood. By using my wits, I take money from rich people for the benefit of others."

Greenstein's comment on poker is the answer to the age-old question, "Who is the best poker player in the world?" Barry Greenstein's answer is, "No one. Nobody plays his or her best every day. No player is the best in all forms of poker, against all groups of opponents, on an everyday basis. Even in your poker circle, you are not going to be the best all the time. Just try to play well and manage well."

His advice is:

"Overconfidence can lead to carelessness in decision-making. [Author's note: Remember, poker is about making the correct decisions.] The poker gods can provide a run of bad cards that will make anyone look foolish."

Russ Hamilton

Russ Hamilton won the world championship in 1994. Winning the World Series main event is the dream of any poker player, but in 1994 the honor was made even more special because it was Binion's Horseshoe Casino's twenty-fifth anniversary. For the silver anniversary owner, Jack Binion announced that the winner would be playing not only for the $1 million prize and the gold bracelet, but also, in celebration of Binion's twenty-fifth year, the new world champion would also win his weight in sterling silver bars. Russ tells the story. "Every year when the main event got to heads up, the tournament director would call Jack Binion so he could make the arrangements to bring the money in and watch the heads-up action. That year when he received the call, his first question was, 'How much do they weigh?'" Hamilton continues, "The tournament director told him, 'One hundred forty pounds and three hundred thirty pounds!' I'm pretty sure that year that Jack Binion was rooting for the man who weighed only one hundred forty pounds. They never expected the winner to weigh over three hundred pounds." (Since 1994 Hamilton has lost over one hundred seventy pounds!) "After I won, I had my choice if I wanted the silver bars or cash. I chose the ten-pound silver bars. They had to order three more! They had only thirty on hand! To tell the truth, I actually weighed three hundred seventy but their scales didn't go that high, and I was embarrassed to tell them. So, Binion's still owes me four silver bars!"

In addition to Hamilton's success at the poker tables, he was a professional blackjack player prior to 1990. He turned to poker after he was invited not to return to many casinos to play blackjack. He has been called one of the best all-around card players in the world.

Russ Hamilton discusses a few of the differences in playing limit hold'em and no-limit. "The biggest difference to me is the starting hands. I can play a lot more hands in no-limit because after the flop I can win a *lot* of money with a hand like J-9 suited, more than I can win in limit hold'em with the same hand. You have to start with only good quality hands in limit because you are limited to what you can win after the flop. You won't flop enough hands in limit poker with the J-9 to make it a worthwhile hand to play. In limit, start only with good quality starting hands and play them aggressively. In no-limit you can start with a lot of different hands as long as you play good after the flop, and this only comes with a lot of playing time and experience. You have to be able to steal in no-limit and that means having a lot of heart. It's not for the weak-hearted!"

Linda Johnson

Linda Johnson went to work at the post office in 1975 and by 1980 had climbed the ladder of success to a very high-paying job. She was next in line to become a postmaster, a unique position for a woman. There was only one obstacle—she was absolutely enthralled and passionate about the game of poker. She gave herself some challenges, passed them, and decided to become a professional poker player. She has been a trailblazer for other female professional poker players ever since.

In 1992, due to a series of circumstances and what Linda deems fate, she along with two partners bought *Card Player* magazine and Card Player Cruises. She spearheaded the World Poker Conferences, the World Poker Player's Conferences, and was a cofounder of the Tournament Director's Association.

In 1997, Johnson became only the second woman to win an open-field event at the World Series of Poker. She was a strong driving force behind the original idea for the World Poker Tour and today serves as the color commentator for the nationally televised show. Due to her many contributions to the world of poker, her peers have hailed her as the "First Lady of Poker."

Her best advice in no-limit is:

"Don't bet more than you have to to get the job done. For example, if the blinds are $50-$100 and you are trying to steal the blinds, you can attempt it by raising somewhere between $300 and $400. There is no need to move all in for $2,000 and risk having someone wake up with two aces and bust you."

Howard Lederer

Howard Lederer discovered poker at age eighteen when he found the poker game in the back room of his favorite chess club. His passion quickly changed from chess to poker. He was hooked; however, in those early days, he admits to going home broke nine times out of ten. In the mid-eighties, he honed his no-limit skill playing at the Mayfair Club in New York with some of today's top players. To continue his poker progression he moved to Las Vegas in 1993. He considers no-limit hold'em both exciting and terrifying. He is quoted as saying, "There is nothing like the thrill of playing at a big-money final table."

He makes many appearances at final tables on the tournament circuit, claiming in recent years two World Poker Tour titles, one Bellagio Five Star Classic Championship, and two World Series titles along with the coveted gold bracelets, the ultimate goal of all serious tournament poker players.

He is considered to be one of the most respected and consistently winning professional poker players in the world today. Because his winning poker style is often called "intellectual" and he is a great teacher, he has been labeled the "Poker Professor."

Professor Lederer's tips are on tells and razz:

"When you are trying to read opponents, study their hands. Players are always conscious of their face, but they actually will give more away with their hands. If you closely study how a player puts chips in the pot when he has a big hand as opposed to when he is bluffing, you will have a huge edge. You will be able get a great read while ignoring a lot of unreliable information that might come from studying their faces.

"Good drawing hands are actually the favorite in razz on fifth street. With two cards to come, if you have the better four-card hand, you can raise against even a better five-card hand if you are drawing smoother. An example would be if your opponent bets with 9-8-6 (X-X) on board. You can raise with K-6-5-3-2. Your 6 low draw is the favorite against the made 9 low and the possible 8 low draw."

Tom McEvoy hails from Grand Rapids, Michigan, giving him the nickname in the poker world of "Grand Rapids Tom." He married there and had a family while working as an accountant. He found this normal life boring and stifling. He had learned to play poker at his grandmother's knee when he was only five years old, and after several visits to Las Vegas to play poker (once he was all grown up) he decided he had enough talent to become a professional poker player. He made that decision in 1979 and never looked back. He won the world championship in 1983 and was the first player ever to play and win the main event from a satellite victory (satellite play was just getting started in the early eighties.) He has a total of four WSOP bracelets. He considers himself a tournament specialist. His list of wins, places, and shows is so long he probably can't remember them all. Most notably he has been in the winner's circle of the WSOP eighteen other times. Over the years as he educated himself on the best way to win at poker, he began to share this information with his friends and fans. This resulted in a series of poker books almost as long as his tournament record. As of this writing, Tom has twelve poker books out. I personally call him the Professor because he has taught me so much.

Many have used his original quote on the luck factor in tournament competition:

"In tournament play you have to have developed the skill to survive long enough in order to give yourself the opportunity to get lucky. If you win a tournament, you will have gotten lucky...more than once!"

Daniel Negreanu

This young Canadian, born in 1974, started playing poker at the age of fifteen and moved to Las Vegas to play poker full time as soon as he was of legal age. In 1998, at age twenty-three, he won the first World Series event that he'd ever played—the Pot-Limit Hold'em Tournament. Early in his poker career, between 1997 and 1999, he won more than any other player on the circuit during that time span. Daniel is considered one of the top tournament players in the world who also excels in cash games. He has been known to be one of the more outspoken players in the world, often tackling complicated poker issues and showing no fear of rocking the boat. Daniel Negreanu is one of the most familiar people in poker and rightfully so. His success is enormous, his talent is unrivaled, and his personality is unforgettable. In 2004, Daniel won the *Card Player* magazine's Tournament Player of the Year award and the World Series of Poker's Player of the Year award. Daniel started 2005 as second on the World Poker Tours all-time money list with his winnings topping $4 million in that series of events only. His total final table appearances and championships are too numerous to list.

His tips and suggestions are:

"There is one key difference that is often over-looked. Optimal play on the flop differs greatly between limit and no-limit hold'em. In limit, it's important to pound, pound, pound with top pair while in no-limit you need to proceed cautiously on the flop. Top pair is a strong hand worth multiple bets in limit hold'em, but in no-limit if all of your money goes in and you are called—you usually are dead. So, with that bit of information, you should adjust your strategy and try to take the lead as often as possible in limit hold'em while looking to trap a little more often in no-limit.

"Bring back the limp!" Daniel declares. "Every-one believes that to play no-limit correctly you must always be raising or reraising." He suggests, "In shorthanded or heads-up play, bring back the limp because you never know what that flop might bring."

Scotty Nguyen

Scotty Nguyen (pronounced "win," how appropriate!) arrived in the United States in 1979, a refugee from South Vietnam, one of the original "boat people." He has always said that becoming a professional poker player was his dream, his goal, and that it was in his blood. He began as a poker dealer and learned many of the skills necessary to become a great poker player. He is a lady's man and known to call everyone "baby," the word he ends most of his sentences with.

In 1998, when he won the world championship, he is quoted as saying to his opponent Kevin McBride, "You call this one and it's all over, baby." McBride called and it was all over. McBride had called thinking that playing the full house on the board was going to get him half the pot, but Scotty had a 9 in his hand, giving him a larger full house. Scotty earned the title and a million dollars. He is also among the highest-earning tournament players of all time. Scotty's list of titles is lengthy, including three other WSOP bracelets in addition to his world championship. He is one of the most aggressive poker players playing today and always plays to win, which is why he has one of the highest total tournament winnings of all time. Although his superconfident and aggressive style sometimes gets him into trouble, it also is the reason he has so many titles.

Scotty's tip was surprisingly on table manners rather than strategy. The subject is obviously important to him. "Play nice. No need to be mean to anybody, baby; no need to be rude. Everybody should just play nice and never be ugly to each other. Play poker with class, baby."

Greg "Fossilman" Raymer

Greg Raymer seemed to come out of nowhere and has taken the poker world by storm. His nickname "Fossilman" comes from the fossils he collects, some of which he uses as card cappers at the table. In 2000, Raymer burst onto the poker scene, a virtual unknown, by making the final table at the World Poker Finals and finishing in third place. In 2004, on the heels of the unbelievable WSOP victory of Chris Moneymaker, who won his seat online for $40 and went on to become the world champion, Greg also won his seat at the same online poker site, Poker Stars. Two amateur players winning the world championship changed the face of competitive poker forever. It was now proven that an everyday man, a regular guy, could win the gold. It was Raymer's third time to play the main event and he proceeded to defeat a field of 2,576 players. He won over $5 million for his first-place finish, which was the single largest cash prize for a poker tournament ever. The win put him at the top of the most all-time money won list for the WSOP. He followed up in 2005 by almost doing the impossible, when he came in twenty-fifth out of a field of over fifty-six hundred in the WSOP main event. Greg has a well-deserved reputation as a nice guy both on and off the poker table. He is a family man who has put his full-time job as a patent attorney for a large pharmaceutical company on hold while he pursues his career as a professional poker player.

The famous Fossilman has several tips:

"My number one tip: Never gamble with money you can't afford to lose. If you do this, nothing else is really that big of a deal.

"Don't just buy and zip through a poker book. Buy the best poker books, and really study them. Spend lots of time on each page, and really think about all the aspects of what the author is saying. There is no cheaper way to learn how to play better.

"In limit poker, you need to play tight early and loose late. Early in a hand, unless you're sure you should be playing the given hand, be heavily inclined to fold. Late in the hand, unless you're sure that folding is correct, be heavily inclined to call or raise."

Mike Sexton

Mike Sexton has been involved in the poker industry for more than twenty-five years. Before he became a professional player, Mike attended Ohio State University on a gymnastics scholarship. After graduation and a stint in the army, he stayed in North Carolina, got married, and worked real jobs for four years, including teaching ballroom dancing (Mike's hobby is dancing, and he is as smooth on the dance floor as he is at a poker table). At that time he began playing in home games and in late 1977 decided to quit his job and try playing poker for a living, which he did for over twenty years. He moved to Las Vegas in 1985. Mike was in on the ground floor of the World Poker Tour (see the introduction). He has gained celebrity status by cohosting the WPT with Vince Van Pattern on the Travel Channel. He writes regularly for *Card Player* magazine and *Gambling Times,* and served as a host and consultant for the largest online poker cardroom, Party Poker. It was some of Mike's promotional ideas that skyrocketed Party Poker to its top two poker site status.

Mike is known by many from the "old poker world" for being the founder (and the developer) of the Tournament of Champions. This unique event, held once a year, allowed any player from anywhere in the world who won a sizable tournament during the previous year to compete. This field of champion players produced the "best of the best" (and a pretty hefty prize pool). Unfortunately, this terrific event lasted only three years, but it was very well received. Mike says, "It could be back."

With the Tournament of Champions, the grand success of Party Poker under the direction of Sexton, and the change in the world that resulted from the World Poker Tour, Mike Sexton is known as one of the greatest promoters of poker in history.

Mike was also successful in his days as a professional poker player. An excellent tournament player since 1989, he won or found himself in the winner's circle on a multitude of occasions. Most notably, he was in the money a total of thirty-two times at the WSOP and won his first bracelet in the seven-card stud high-low split event.

Mike's advice is to new players and to anyone considering playing poker for a living:

"In poker and life, winning takes effort. I recommend you read and study poker books prior to playing for serious money. Get the fundamentals down and then practice, practice, practice. Of course, I would recommend my book, *Shuffle Up and Deal.*

"The biggest mistake amateurs make is that they play too many hands and call their money off too much. Good players know when to 'get away from a hand' and bad players don't. Remember, the most profitable play in poker is to fold. If you have any aspirations of becoming a professional player, you better love the game. I don't mean 'like' to play poker, I mean 'love' to play."

Dr. Max Stern

Dr. Max Stern practiced medicine in Costa Rica and played poker in private clubs and weekly home games for many years. During this time, Stern, his wife Maria, and many of their Costa Rican poker pals visited Las Vegas regularly and always during the World Series of Poker. He eventually retired to Las Vegas where he continues to play poker professionally. He has numerous wins, places, and shows on the poker circuit to his credit. Most notably are three WSOP bracelets and the most special of the three bracelets is the one he won in 1997, which happened to be the same year his wife won her first WSOP championship, making them the first and only husband and wife couple ever to win world titles in the same year. Max won in seven-card stud eight-or-better and Maria in seven-card stud. Stern collaborated with Linda Johnson and Tom McEvoy on the book *Championship Stud.*

Dr. Stern is also a world champion no-limit player. His advice to you is famous and has been claimed by many. It is simple and to the point. "Sometimes in no-limit hold'em, in order to live, you have to be willing to die."

Robert Williamson

Robert Williamson enjoys traveling all over the world to play poker. His words to live by are "carpe diem"—seize the day! He literally is half the man he was when he first started playing professional poker, having lost more than two hundred pounds. He states, "I am much, much more vibrant these days. I used to need ten to twelve hours of sleep a day. Now, I sleep about six hours, so it has given me more hours in the day. My energy level is incredible. I was missing control in that one area of my life, but now I have control of all areas. I can play longer hours because I have more stamina. I am happier with my life and confident that I will be around for a long time."

Williamson's list of money finishes in major tournaments is almost as long as the Mississippi River. He has made a dozen in the money finishes in the World Series of Poker, including two second-place and two third-place wins as of this writing. He notes that he was thrilled to take home the gold by winning his first gold bracelet in the $5,000 Pot-Limit Omaha event in 2002. His goal is to win many more World Series bracelets.

His poker tip brings up a great point that is often overlooked:

"Don't play over your head. Whether it is the limits you play or the competition you play against, don't play over your head. Pick and choose carefully for your best results."

Another Williamson tip is on tipping:

"If you want to make sure that the cocktail waitress or important other waiter (person) in your life pays close attention to your every need, make sure your first tip (gratuity) of the night is extra (very) generous. Don't worry, if they are making a living at waiting on people, they will realize real quickly that you do not mind paying generously for good service (and it will normally continue throughout the night—sometimes the whole weekend—and if you are really fortunate, the entire week!!!). This is a proven principle because I love great service!"

One last note: If you are interested in researching the history of any poker player's tournament results, go to www.thehendonmob.com for in-depth player statistics on all major poker competitions.

Bibliography

Ace on the River: An Advanced Poker Guide, Barry Greenstein.

Awesome Profits: From Kitchen Poker Table to Tournament Final Table, George Elias.

Caro's Book of Poker Tells, Mike Caro.

Championship Hold'em, T. J. Cloutier and Tom McEvoy.

Championship No-Limit and Pot-Limit Hold'em, T. J. Cloutier and Tom McEvoy.

Championship Omaha, T. J. Cloutier and Tom McEvoy.

Championship Stud: 7-Card Stud, Stud/8, Razz, Max Stern, Tom McEvoy, and Linda Johnson

Doyle Brunson's Super System, Doyle Brunson.

Doyle Brunson's Super System 2, Doyle Brunson.

Get the Edge at Low-Limit Texas Hold'em, Bill Burton.

Internet Texas Hold'em: Winning Strategies from an Internet Pro, Matthew Hilger.

Harrington on Hold'em Expert Strategy for No-Limit Tournaments: Strategic Play (Vol. 1), Dan Harrington.

Killer Poker Online: Crushing the Internet Game, John Vorhaus.

MsPoker: Up Close and Personal, Susie Isaacs.

Omaha Hi-Lo Poker (Eight or Better) How to Win at the Lower Limits, Shane Smith.

Poker: The Real Deal, Phil Gordon.

Shuffle Up and Deal, Mike Sexton.

About the Author

Susie Isaacs is best known for being the first woman to win the World Series of Poker ladies' championship back-to-back in 1996 and 1997. In 1998, she placed tenth in the World Series of Poker $10,000 event, vying for the $1 million first prize. Isaacs became the second woman in history to accomplish such an outstanding finish. She is a professional tournament poker player who has won various titles and placed in the money numerous times over the past fifteen years, including winning the first Queen of Hearts Tournament at the Bicycle Casino in Los Angeles, winning the Best All Round award at the Ladies Crystal Open in Reno, and winning first place at the Orleans Open in Las Vegas. Isaacs was voted in to play on the 2005 Pro Poker Tour of the World Poker Tour.

In addition to her career as a professional poker player, Isaacs has written a regular column and feature stories for *Casino Journal, Strictly Slots, Poker Digest, Poker Player* newspaper, and *Card Player* magazines. Currently she is a regular columnist for *Women's Poker Player* magazine, *Top Pair* magazine, and the *American Poker Player* magazine, which features her popular column "Chip Chatter."

Isaacs is a recognized expert on the subject of poker. Nationally, Isaacs has appeared in *Card Player* magazine, "Geraldo Rivera Reports from Las Vegas: The American Fantasy," and "Behind the Scene at the World Series of Poker" on the Discovery Channel.

She made a guest appearance on the World Poker Tour and was seen on ESPN's "Ladies' Night" segment at the World Series of Poker, having made the final table of the ladies' world championship (again).

In 2005, she played on Jim Woods's team on the GSN poker series, *Poker Royale,* when the James Woods Gang faced off with the Unabombers.

In Las Vegas, Isaacs has received media coverage in the *Review Journal Business Section,* "Nevadan at Work," Larry Grossman's radio talk show, *You Can Bet On It,* and Las Vegas Channel 13 news, *Inside Las Vegas,* in a segment titled "Winning Over Women."

In 1999, Isaacs published her first book, *MsPoker: Up Close and Personal.* She is presently working on a new book: *Queens Can Beat Kings: A Woman's Guide to Poker.* She has also written *MsPoker: I'm Not Bluffing,* a two-book series, and an autobiography titled *Me and My Mama.* She has a novel entitled *Poker Is Skill, Life Is the Gamble* in the works.

Susie also has a line of poker jewelry (www.susieisaacs.com).